THE HEART OF A KING

—THE LEADERSHIP MEASURE OF THE JOSEPH-DANIEL CALLING —

by

Morris E. Ruddick

Copyright © 2010 by Morris E. Ruddick

The Heart of a King
The Leadership Measure of the Joseph-Daniel Calling
by Morris E. Ruddick

Printed in the United States of America

ISBN 9781615797691

All rights reserved solely by the author. The author guarantees all contents are original and do not infringe upon the legal rights of any other person or work. No part of this book may be reproduced in any form without the permission of the author. The views expressed in this book are not necessarily those of the publisher.

Unless otherwise indicated, Bible quotations are taken from The New King James Version of the Bible. Copyright © 1979, 1980, 1982 by Thomas Nelson, Inc.

Co-Published by Xulon Press and Global Initiatives Foundation

www.xulonpress.com

Bill & Linda,
With every blessing,
Morris

ALSO AVAILABLE BY MORRIS RUDDICK

THE JOSEPH-DANIEL CALLING: Facilitating the Release of the Wealth of the Wicked

GOD'S ECONOMY, ISRAEL AND THE NATIONS: Discovering God's Ancient Kingdom Principles of Business and Wealth

TABLE OF CONTENTS

Chapter	Page

DEDICATION and ACKNOWLEDGEMENTS xi

PREFACE xv

    SECTION I: THE SETTING AND CHALLENGE 21

1. THE NEW THING 23

2. THE VALLEY OF SHADOWS 30

3. OPPORTUNITY ENABLERS..36

4. SPIRITUAL CLUTTER..43

5. DISCERNING THE KINGDOM 53

6. THE MATURITY MANTLE..59

7. THE COST OF THE PATHWAY 67

SECTION II: ADDRESSING THE REALITIES 75

8. THE SNARE IN SUCCESS 77
9. SPIRITUAL INTOXICATION..86
10. THE WEALTH TRANSFER DYNAMIC 92
11. HIGH CALLING REALITIES 100
12. THE THRONE OF DESTRUCTION 107
13. THE SWIRL...118
14. WHEN INIQUITY STOPS ITS MOUTH 128

SECTION III: DEFINING THE ISSUES 139

15. WITHOUT PRETENSE..141
16. THE MOLD..147
17. HONOR FALLEN SHORT...156
18. HONOR AND INTEGRITY 163
19. PRIORITY AND OPPORTUNITY.................................170
20. PIERCING THE VEIL...177
21. PREVAILING 185

SECTION IV: EMBRACING THE MANDATE 193

22. THE MANTLE OF POWER 195

23. THIS IS THE GENERATION 202

24. THE CORPORATE COMMUNITY 209

25. THE MOST HUMBLE..215

26. THE DIVIDING ASUNDER..223

27. THE LEADERSHIP MEASURE 229

28. THE HEART OF A KING...236

APPENDIX

The Author...245

Contact Information 247

DEDICATION

Dedicating a book is a very personal matter. I've been enriched and blessed by those I count as my friends and family. Many names have come to mind as I've prayed about this dedication. As a sequel to my two previous books addressing the calling of marketplace leaders, my previous dedications have targeted ones who have served a special role in my life.

For this book, I would like to give focus to those whose leadership in the Body is out of the ordinary. First, there are a handful of leaders in lands of persecution, where we have worked, whose dedication embraces sacrifice and commitment unheard of in the West. They stand as a model for the topic addressed by this book.

I also want to dedicate this effort to the modern pioneers of faith, who have left the comforts of their homeland to immigrate and serve as believers in the Land of Promise, Israel. They are inextinguishable sparks igniting the prophetic light of Israel, soon to be taken to all the nations

Finally, this book is dedicated to the emerging generation of Josephs and Daniels who are breaking the mold and facilitating this move of God in the marketplace.

ACKNOWLEDGEMENTS

For reviewing this manuscript and providing keen insights I would like to acknowledge and express my deep appreciation to Dr. Bill Bolton, Barbara Fox, David Works and Wayne Newcomb.

I also want to acknowledge those who have invested their time on my behalf in interceding for me and for the fulfillment of God's purposes in my life. I'm deeply humbled by this type of sacrifice coming from a long list of dear friends, family and co-laborers in the Lord.

PREFACE

In extraordinary times, knowing-what-to-do takes something more. That something more is what distinguishes true leadership. If we can just get the door sufficiently open to get a glimmer from God, it will be enough. It will be that something more that makes a difference. The following chapters are a collection of "glimmers" that I've drawn from my time of prayer, of seeking the Lord for answers to the times.

This book targets a select audience of men and women of God called to be the movers and shakers for the times upon us. Much like Joseph and Daniel, their destinies come with a high cost. Likewise, the pathway is narrow. The calling is one that follows the description of Jesus' followers in Acts 17 of *"turning the world upside down."*

This volume is a sequel to my two previous books about this calling. Reading "The Joseph-Daniel Calling" and "God's Economy, Israel and the Nations" is strongly recommended before savoring the "glimmers" contained in this book.

The defining dimension to this calling is the heart of a king. With the need to grasp the setting and face the realities, what follows provides a glimpse into what incorporates the heart of a king in God's kingdom. The heart of a king is not patterned after the ways of the world. There are realities to the calling and the cost it upholds. There are realities to the times.

The Keys of Release

Having recently arrived back from an agenda in Southeast Asia, spiritually I was depleted and spent. A key part of our effort targets lands of persecution. We had been on the go, almost non-stop for over four months; encountering a vast array of spiritual hurdles and challenges, along with almost 60,000 miles traveled during that time frame. So with our return, all I wanted to do was veg out and recover. Yet hardly out of jet lag, I received an unexpected and incredibly difficult intercessory assignment.

As I embraced this mission, in the spirit I found myself being led into a deep, dark place with the keys to unlock shackles and lead out ones who had been immobilized in their quests to reach their high-callings. Night after night the Lord showed me ones I have been acquainted with, who bear high callings, who spiritually had been stymied along their pathways. Not due to any fault of their own, in one way or another, each had faced seemingly insurmountable barriers or become casualties in the spiritual battles raging.

One example was my dear friend David Works. In December of 2007, the Works family became victims of a tragedy-beyond-words that took place in their church parking lot. Attacked by a deranged young man firing an assault rifle, two of his teenage daughters were killed and David seriously wounded. (http://www.GoneInAHeartbeat.com)

Understandably following this tragic event, David and his family had found a safe place in their coming to terms with its impact. However, having known and spent years praying with David prior to this tragedy, I knew this safe place lacked the vision of his calling as a modern-day Joseph. So I recently challenged him on reclaiming his significant calling.

David began doing just that. Then midway through my intense prayer initiative, David dropped by with some news. The day prior was the second anniversary of the tragedy. His church had held a special memorial service. What David eagerly shared was a newspaper article about the memorial service. In big headline print were the words: "Our Dream is Coming Back." Indeed, his dream and high calling are coming back.

There were other friends and associates the Lord showed me to target during this unusual time of prayer; who spiritually experienced set-backs from the mark of the high calling on their lives. In each case, they have been leaders. In each case, they were at a critical threshold in terms of embracing a new and key dimension to their callings. Some bore the callings to release still others; such as the leaders we've worked with in Asia, Africa and the Middle East.

The Realities of the Spiritual Environment

As I progressed through these extremely intense encounters in prayer, I became keenly aware of the environment those being released would be reentering.

The best way I can describe this spiritual atmosphere is that it is filled with danger, duplicity and intrigue; not unlike the era during 16th century England in the years following Henry VIII's death, when there was a vicious and deadly quest for power from within the Tudor Court. It was a time when the lust for power capitalized on and perverted otherwise genuine leadership efforts. It was a time when it took great courage to put your hand to the plow and keep it there.

Similarly, in today's spiritual atmosphere, in keeping with the unusual developments underway in global seats of power; I became very conscious of a jockeying for power taking place within circles of believers. The generation now assuming their mantles face a toxic spiritual setting perhaps summed up best by a book title I recently came across: "Hemlock at Vespers."

The Courage to Come Forth

Like the understandable response of my friend David, there is a safe place, which is sometimes needed to regroup and heal. However, while it may be safe from certain levels of the dangers, it also maintains the enticements and protective machinations of the soul response, hindering what had begun in the Spirit as the pathway of the high calling.

The issue involves looking back rather than forward; of being immobilized from facing the realities and embracing the high calling. The message of this book is for those reaching for the mark, whose aim is nothing short of completing in the Spirit what was begun in the Spirit.

The Heart of a King
There indeed is a great battle taking place within the Body today. It reflects a transfer of the mantle between generations. With that transfer is a struggle reflecting the fine line between the good and the perfect will of God; between the soul and the spirit; the measures defining kingdom success; and the venturing forth from the safe places into the places of risk that carry the potential of impacting eternity. It is a calling of leadership for those with a heart of a king.

What's key in the parallel of the Tudor Court power-struggle to today's spiritual turbulence was what followed, when England became united under the leadership of Queen Elizabeth I. Then came a time when Philip II of Spain, saw his empire as the worldly arm of the Roman Catholic Church. Seeing himself as the sword to undo the Reformation and reunite Europe in a single faith, Philip became obsessed with conquering England. Henry VIII had led England out of the church. Now his daughter Elizabeth was defending her father's reformation. Philip, honing his blade in 1581, was at their shores with his 'invincible Armada.'

England's greatest weapon, however, was the selfless leadership of its queen. Now in her mid-fifties, she had ruled England for thirty years and was skilled in the use of power. She knew how to use the crown, and, in that hour of national peril, how to mobilize her people. Unlike the divisions created by the ambitions of unworthy aspirants to the power of the throne during the interim after her father's death, Elizabeth united her people to stand against the Spanish invasion.

While the Armada was still off England, dramatically riding up on a white horse, Queen Elizabeth, known among the people as "Good Queen Bess," reviewed the army and addressed them with these stirring words:

"Let tyrants fear. I have always so behaved myself that, under God, I have placed my chiefest strength and safeguard in the loyal hearts and goodwill of my subjects; and therefore I am come amongst you, resolved, in the midst of the heat of the battle, to live or die amongst you, to lay down for my God, and for my kingdom, and for my people, my honor and my blood, even in the dust. I know I have the body of a weak and feeble woman, but I have the heart and stomach of a king, and of a king of England too, and

think foul scorn that Parma or Spain or any prince of Europe should dare to invade the borders of my realm; to which, rather than any dishonor shall grow by me, I myself will take up arms, I myself will be your general, judge and rewarder of every one of your virtues in the field." (Source: Winston Churchill, "Churchill's History of the English Speaking Peoples," Barnes & Noble, 1995)

Good Queen Bess' words exude the true heart of a king. Indeed, let tyrants fear, along with the misguided and the lawless interlopers whose human efforts impede the true work of the Spirit. A line has been crossed. The stakes are far higher than in the days of Elizabeth. The clash of all ages is before us. These are times of monumental change.

These are times that cry out for true leadership in the Body; the type that unites and mobilizes. It comes from a calling not to be treated lightly or with presumption. It is a leadership of sacrifice, but one that is not reckless. The goal of the high calling involves lethal realities and demands a wisdom that avoids the entrapments and diversions.

Those bearing this mantle have been prepared by God. They are unwilling to acquiesce to the safe places that fall short; or be seduced by the rule of power or the rule of profit that lures those called by His Name into the intrigues and games played by the world.

They are a remnant whose calling is directly from God; not presumption, ambition or any other quest emerging from the heart of man. It is a calling that excludes the pretenders, wannabes, interlopers and tyrants. The heart and identity defining this remnant is inexorably tied to God.

These are the ones with the leadership mantle of Joseph and Daniel, who are facing the realities, paying the cost and faithfully stewarding their callings of bringing forth God's Kingdom. These are the ones who will themselves receive the keys to release His Kingdom in their domains. These are the ones with the heart of a King. These are the ones for whom this book has been written.

GLIMMERS
...of Kingdom insights for the times

In extraordinary times, there are no ordinary answers
...and sacrifice will mark the pathway

When freedom flounders; truth stabilizes
When tyranny undermines; liberty unmasks
When self-interest entices; commitment perseveres
When disorder advances; wisdom redirects
When fear invades; courage takes its stand
When destiny calls; true leaders arise.

SECTION I:

THE SETTING AND CHALLENGE

CHAPTER 1

THE NEW THING

"Behold, I am doing a new thing! Now it springs forth; do you not perceive it and will you not give heed to it? I will even make a way in the wilderness and rivers in the desert." Isaiah 43:19 Amplified

The time it takes a generation to get it together with what God is doing, too often results in the "new thing" already becoming outmoded. However, times of dramatic change bring another dynamic into play. The tempo is accelerated. Cycles become more prominent and erratic. People adapt more quickly.

The rules have changed. Old models are falling short. Challenging times demand something more. The spiritual dynamics that Joseph the patriarch employed in the world of his day to turn crisis into opportunity, represent a parallel for the times at hand.

As the rules change, defining opportunity means operating beyond the ordinary. It means avoiding the status quo, the trendy and the herd-instinct that panics. It means restoring foundations proven to bridge turmoil. The enduring foundations are adrift. Historically, virtue and God-centeredness formed the basis for our liberty. Slippage from these fundamentals has opened the gates to disorder and the unexpected.

Yet despite the disorder, God is not only ahead of the power curve, He is re-establishing age-old foundations. These restored foundations will release a new thing. This "new thing" will be hidden to those whose bearings are outside the basis that God outlined for society. The new thing will reflect the principles Joseph employed to avert disaster. It will employ Kingdom principles Jesus imparted that will navigate a narrow pathway through reversals and turbulence the world will see.

The shift to the new will be at a strategic level. It will not be based on past patterns of "success" defined by the world's standards.

Joseph's role with Pharaoh was not only prophetic in nature. It redefined the way things had been done. For centuries the Church has operated on the premise of the spiritual being the spiritual and the natural being the natural, without the two intersecting. While faith clearly changes things, our operational precepts and alignments have been such that they have yet to bring the level of societal change that we refer to as transformation. The foundation for the new thing must move deeper. It involves influence.

Within the spiritual arena *influence* is defined by spiritual or God-centered criteria. Within the natural or "secular" arena, influence is defined by success that most generally is based on wealth or extraordinary shrewdness.

The Process of Change

This foundation has got to change. It is the deception that subtly decries "we have to be like everyone else to be heard."

By understanding where we are heading, we can better discern the pathway defining how we need to be proceeding. Isaiah 60 describes the shift of all ages. Israel and God's chosen people, the Jews, are the pivot point. The change outlined in Isaiah 60 will result in "the wealth of the seas" being turned to Israel.

"Nations will come to your light, and kings to the brightness of your rising... Then you will see and be radiant, and your heart will thrill and rejoice; because the abundance of the sea will be turned to you, the wealth of the nations will come to you." Isa 60: 3, 5

The influence that has operated through the Jewish people over the ages will come full circle. Isaiah 60 indicates that the best or "the glory" of the nations will swing to Israel. Those resisting will perish. The rage and persecution from the nations described in Psalm 1 will pass and God's chosen people will enter their inheritance — amid the nations of this world.

"Although you have been despised and hated, I will make you the joy of all generations. You will drink the milk of nations and be nursed at royal breasts." Isa 60: 15, 16

God's people, as a people, will no longer be guided by "being like everyone else" or be molded by pathways defined by the world.

The Pathway to the New Thing
The pathway toward the Isaiah 60 shift will embrace the "new thing." The new thing will encompass a shift in dominion and influence. It will move God's people toward *"being the head, rather than the tail."* (Deut 28:13) The standard that has defined influence and authority for the world will revert to the standard that the Jewish people have so tangibly brought to the world over the centuries.

As advisors to kings and merchants, the Jewish people have redefined civilization and the standards for the legal, moral, economic and governmental systems of the world.

While the premises for the change brought about by the Jews has been based on foundations found in the Jewish Torah, the world including the Church today, largely has failed to recognize the dynamics that have been the catalysts effecting that change. The Jewish people have the model. In practice, they are walking Torahs. Even among those considered as "non-observing" or the non-religious, righteous Jews apply with balance the key dynamics needed for the pathway ahead.

These dynamics are at the core of what Jesus referred to as "the Kingdom." These elements, with the pattern unchanged today, are why the Jewish community has been the brunt of the rage and hate of the world over the ages. The reason is that they not only have the answer, they operate according to the answer. It is an answer that spiritually goes against the grain. Against all odds they have and are achieving a dimension of influence and dominion that is far beyond the ordinary.

Once we as the Church, as God's spliced-in people, grasp this pathway, we too will wield the influence and dominion that have been evident over the centuries in the impact made by this extremely small, yet remarkable segment of the world's population. As we embrace these dynamics in traversing this path toward the Isaiah 60 shift, the Church will experience even more of the brunt of hate that has for so long followed the Jewish people.

Entering the Narrow Path

One of the first premises to traveling this pathway is that we are not like everyone else. The standard is not being nice people with high moral ethics who can achieve. That might be the by-product. The standard is the identity we embrace and uphold as being God's people.

As God's people then, we need to operate as a people. We need to reflect the unity that has long defined the Jewish community.

That unity will only manifest by fully embracing God's gift of community. Within pop Christian culture today, a strategy tied to influencing culture has been resurrected from the Charismatic renewal of the early 70s. It is a good, yet somewhat flawed strategy. It is now being referred to as the Seven Mountains of Influence. It incorporates believers penetrating and bringing influence to the spheres of religion, government, business, education, media, the arts and family.

A key area in which this paradigm falls short is that it either equates or replaces "community" with family. Community will incorporate family, but community is too pivotal a dynamic to be redefined by one of its components. This is in no way to detract from the significance of family. However, family outside the community dimension designed by God will face unnecessary hurdles. Likewise, biblical community is watered down by relabeling it simply as "the social" area.

Defining the New-Old Thing

Community is one of the three keys to understanding the dynamic that has operated so uniquely through the Jewish people. The primary key is being God-centered. The final key is operating according to the "entrepreneurial" principle of increase that bleeds into business, technology, government, education, arts and the media. All three are meant to operate together, in balance.

So it is that *God-centered community that brings increase* is the foundation for influence and dominion. It is God-centered community that brings increase that is the pathway for the "new thing."

Joseph, as God's chosen, understood God-centered community that brought increase. Joseph was described by the non-believers around him as being successful in all that he did because God was with him. So it will be for the new generation of Josephs who are embedded in the infrastructures of the world's system. They will redefine and employ opportunity according to this "new," yet very old standard.

Jesus' central purpose was restoration. Restoring this three-fold dynamic to God's original intentions was key. He went to everyday Jewish people and demonstrated how the principles of God's Kingdom rule operated. He explained in parables the people could understand, about the basic principles that incorporated the God-centered community model that brought increase. This is the model established by Abraham.

Jesus came at a time in history when the rule and authority were in the hands of the Romans. The religious hierarchy operated with a misguided influence defined by zeal for their own comfort zones that aligned them with the Roman conquerors. Jesus sternly rejected the elitism, exclusiveness and privilege that were operating within their ranks.

"Jesus said to them, surely tax collectors and harlots will enter the kingdom of God before you. Therefore, the kingdom of God will be taken from you and given to a people bearing the fruits of it. Woe to you, hypocrites! For you shut up the kingdom of heaven against men; for you neither go in yourselves, nor do you allow those who are entering to go in." Matt 21: 28-44; 23:13-14

Today, when we define success by the worldly standards of wealth, power and cleverness, we short-circuit the model established by Abraham. When all we strive for is excellence according to the world's standards, whether in business, government, education, the arts, the media or family; we fail in bringing the societal change that Jesus' Kingdom message intended.

The Model for the New Thing

The model is *God-centered community that brings increase*. The foundation of "increase" is the entrepreneurial. God's DNA is to create, innovate, build and bring increase. Those elements are at the heart of entrepreneurship which, when God is at the center, brings purpose and balance to community.

Community. The world doesn't understand community in the unique way that the Jewish people do. The Church as a rule has only grasped community in part. God-centered community takes care of its own. Those who wield the greatest influence are the community's greatest benefactors. Community is the pathway, the overflow of which spills blessing and positive change into the realm of society around it. God-defined community will attract rather than have to convince. Community will also create discord and backlash from those aligned to the status quo.

God-Centered. Jesus defined the operating principles according to the paradoxes that drive God's Kingdom rule. True life comes by dying to self. We lead by serving. We gain by giving. Order comes from change. Wisdom comes from simplicity. In short, success is defined by humility and service. These are the practical mind-sets required as the community standard for God's rule and authority to prevail. They define and are the source of the incredible societal impact the Jewish people have had across the years.

Increase. Increase as God intended is to benefit the community. When the modern free-enterprise system began in America, it was God-centered and community-oriented. It had its foundations in the Jewish model. Yet over time, it has become increasingly perverted. God is no longer at the center; and community no longer reflects God's rule; but rather a watered-down hijacking based on what was at issue with the Tower of Babel.

So it is that we have entered a time of cyclic turbulence. Yet, there is *a pathway defined by God* that will result in societal transformation. It is a pathway that will yield opportunity and increase, despite impossible odds of adversity.

Defining Opportunity in Times of Change

Defining opportunity in times of economic turmoil demands the avoidance of old mind-sets and practices, especially religious ones. Times of uncertainty must move beyond the fervor and contagion of the crowd. Piercing the veil calls for stepping outside the box of decisions that base the success of future opportunity on patterns and models of the past. The status quo will and must be challenged. Within the Christian sector, the model for the "new thing," must be based on wisdom and revelation from on high, as Pharaoh recognized it in Joseph.

"Can we find such a one as this; a man in whom is the Spirit of God? Inasmuch as God has shown you all this, there is no one as wise and discerning as you are." Genesis 41: 38-39

The new Joseph generation will know what to do in order to bring purposeful change. They will challenge rather than maintain the status quo as they turn adversity into opportunity. They will apply the new model that brings forth an alignment that releases the supernatural; and does not equate the supernatural with magic or the weird. AND they will penetrate the arenas that wield the authority and resources needed through the modern-day Pharaohs they collaborate with.

Throughout history, God's people have been at the forefront of resetting the default button in times of crisis and transition. The world is bearing the fruits of trying to operate without the One who created it all. We can no longer afford to be like everyone else. The time has come to embrace the "new-old thing" and restore the model of God-centered community that brings increase.

"Then you shall again discern between the righteous and the wicked, between one who serves God and one who does not serve Him." Mal 3:18

CHAPTER 2

THE VALLEY OF SHADOWS

"Even though I walk through the valley of the shadow of death, I will fear no evil, for you are with me." Psalm 23:4

Paul explained to the Galatians that *"in the fullness of time, God sent His Son."*

The "fullness of time" Paul referred to was one of chaos and upheaval. It was a time when God's people were without direction, with those wielding the mantle of God's authority using their positions for personal gain. Jesus described them as *"an evil generation."* While mobilizing an unlikely band of followers to pass the baton to, He pointedly judged the religious leaders misusing their positions and authority.

"Surely tax collectors and harlots will enter the Kingdom of God before you. For the Kingdom of God will be taken from you and given to a people bearing the fruits of it." Matthew 21:31, 43

The fullness of time was the passage into monumental change. It was the gateway into a full-scale confrontation between the forces of evil and the power of God.

The Recurring Error

At the foundation of appropriately wielding the Kingdom mantle is our identity in God. Yet over the ages, acquiescing to the world's order of things has been the recurring error of God's people. In the days of Samuel, the people asked for a king, so they might be like everyone else.

The identity struggle morphed and then peaked in Jesus' day, as the Pharisees curried the favor of the Roman power brokers. Even today, we speak of the Kingdom, yet for the most part, we model success after the world's standard; and justify it by being nice people and brandishing a notch-up in our ethical standards. Our identity flounders at a level of trying to be like everyone else.

Covenant with Death

The core conflict between good and evil is at the heart of the identity issue. One of the most deplorable stages in God's people acquiescing to the world's order was the alliance between Ahab and Jezebel. It was an alliance with sorcery that conformed to the world's standard. God's chosen had digressed to the brink of aligning themselves with the bondage of corruption.

It was a time when black was deemed white and white black; when evil was deemed good and good evil. It was a covenant with death, as the power of God and the forces of evil converged in the standoff between Elijah and the prophets of baal. Years later, the prophet Isaiah foretold hard times that would change the order of things.

"Your covenant with death will be annulled and your agreement with Sheol will not stand. When the overflowing scourge passes through — it will be a terror just to understand the report." Isaiah 28: 18-19

The alliance with death creates an illusion from which spiritual realities are masked. It veils the simple truths that confound the wise and replaces them with deceptive buffers that mesmerize God's people into being like everyone else.

You Can't Argue with Success

In his letter to the Romans, Paul referred to zeal without knowledge. Within the Body today are those who cannot be faulted for their lack of zeal. Despite that, decision-circles bearing on the Kingdom embrace the subtle assumption that you can't argue with success. Yet, this was the very premise that resulted in Ahab calling Elijah the *"troubler of Israel."*

Our model for success has not only become distorted, it had lost touch with reality. The subtlety of that distortion is driven by a central premise of free enterprise. Roughly a hundred years ago, an author by the name of Max Weber wrote a short book titled *"The Protestant Ethic and the Spirit of Capitalism."* That book has become the accepted wisdom for almost every business school within American universities. The assertion is that the free enterprise phenomenon is the result of the work ethic and ethical standard applied in the post-reformation era, but especially in the early years in America.

However, the free enterprise system, in its purist sense, was not birthed from the Protestant ethic or the capitalist approach undergirding the formative years in America. It was based on something much, much more. The Protestant ethic and capitalist approach to what became known as "the American dream," was modeled by Abraham, with its principles outlined in the Jewish Torah.

Abraham's model, of a God-centered, entrepreneurial community, forms the basic elements of the Kingdom imparted by Jesus. Based on the dynamic of God at the center and the increase through business that builds community, the Torah outlines all the elements that brought blessing to the economic foundations of the American phenomenon: private ownership, profit, customer relations, employee relations, diligence, liberty, honor, opportunity, trust, charitable righteousness, community responsibility and more.

The Narrow Path and the Valley

The narrow path of the Kingdom, that Jesus spoke of, will take those walking it into what the psalmist describes as the valley of shadows. It represents, to appearances, an uncertain pathway that has a proximity to evil, death and destruction. It portends vulnerabilities. Yet, in reality the valley of shadows navigates the course toward the still waters of God's Kingdom rule.

Moses arrived at that juncture of the narrow path in his encounter with the burning bush. He was hemmed in. There was no going back to his former position as a prince of Egypt. His choice involved risking it all. His calling required a total identity with God and a confrontation from which the exit could only be through a narrow corridor between life and death.

Moses' mantle was not to be like everyone else, but to confront the culture. His mantle was to deliver God's people from their bondage and onto the pathway toward the still waters. *The steps toward that path began with crossing the line on the identity issue into the confrontation of culture in the valley of shadows.*

The illusion today is that the still waters are represented by the American dream or reaching the top of some other comparable system. The other deception is that the still waters referred to by the psalmist are meant to begin on the other side of eternity. In the words of Jesus, *"Let Your Kingdom come here on earth, as it is in heaven."* The still waters reflect the culture when God's Kingdom rule is in operation.

Jesus came to restore the order of God's Kingdom rule. He refocused the priorities back to God's original mandate of dominion: of God's people ruling over the work of His hands in cooperation with Him. The central theme of what Jesus imparted to His disciples was how to reestablish, on earth, the operation of God's Kingdom rule. He passed on the keys to breaking the bondage of corruption. Nothing less would do it.

The Culture Conflict

The true operation of the Kingdom has always been and is supernatural. It pivots on our unique identity in God and the paradoxical, Kingdom order that runs counter to the way of the world. In our weakness, His power is made manifest. Honor comes from humility. We are to love our enemies and pray for those who abuse us. At the heart of true community are trust and the dynamic of charitable righteousness-tz'dakah. True leadership is found in service; dying to personal ambition is the gateway into genuine life; generosity leads to gain, and wisdom comes from simplicity.

For both the identity issue and restoring Kingdom order, culture is foundational. The Kingdom is the original blueprint, not the other way around. Without God fully at the center, the culture will be a flawed counterfeit, a shadow of the original that entices God's people to conform to the world's standard.

The issue evolves around authority; the restoration of God's authority on earth as it is in heaven. The Joseph calling is not about being like everyone else; it is not about becoming king of the mountain. The story of Joseph represented a most unlikely, yet desired result of this clash of cultures. In this most extraordinary encounter, Pharaoh acquiesced his authority to Joseph, and honored God by completely entrusting this slave/prisoner with his authority, because he recognized the authority of God operating through Joseph.

Then, generations later, after God's people had been totally assimilated into Egyptian society, the Lord said to Moses, *"When you go back to Egypt, do before Pharaoh all the wonders I have put in your hand."* Nothing less than confronting the culture and its authority structure would break the bondage.

Unveiling the Shadows

As the "fullness of time," in which Jesus arrived, reached its juncture, it brought a most pivotal confrontation. This confrontation unveiled the shadows masking the culture of the Kingdom and the mingling of the religious and the world's order. The culture of the religious and the worldly power brokers was an alliance of death, the intent of which was to assimilate and absorb God's people.

At the heart of Jesus' confrontation with the religious leaders bearing the mantle of God's authority were the words: *"you neither understand the scriptures nor the power of God."* The grasp and balance of both is necessary for the operation of God's Kingdom rule.

The restoration of authority from Jesus' confrontation with death restored the mantle of God's Kingdom rule to God's people. With this mantle, those wielding the Kingdom model would bring the transforming hope and change described by Paul in Romans: *"for all creation longs for the revealing of the sons of God, that it might be delivered from the bondage of corruption."* It is the mantle that penetrates the veil of culture.

The necessity of the confrontation is reflected in Jesus' words: *"From the days of John the Baptist until now, the Kingdom of heaven suffers violence and the violent take it by force."* Entrance into the Kingdom was not only out of the box, but beyond the standards of religious tradition. It is the door to those willing to step beyond the standards of conformity and the world's distorted view of success.

The Time of the End

From the fullness of time when Jesus released the Kingdom mantle, we now approach the *"time of the end"* described in Daniel 12: *"In the time of the end, many will be purified and refined, but the wicked will do wickedly and none of the wicked will understand, but the wise will understand."*

Before us is a narrow pathway through the valley. Like previous cultural encounters between evil and the power of God, it marks a time of God's people bringing change.

Our cultural identity as citizens of the Kingdom is tied to traversing the valley of shadows. Jesus spoke of the turbulence that would manifest as the time of the end approaches. Globally, those confused from the conformity standard are looking to recover from the recent downturn. However, there is a second dip yet to manifest.

The pathway is deeper into the valley. The cost involves everything. It is a time to touch things lightly. Yet it is the path marked by His presence that will release new beginnings. It is where the shadows disperse. The valley is where the birthing will take place. The valley of shadows marks the Kingdom alignment on the pathway to still waters.

"The Son of Man will send out His angels, and they will gather out of His kingdom all things that offend, and those who practice lawlessness, and will cast them into the furnace of fire. Then the righteous will shine forth as the sun in the kingdom of their Father." Matthew 13: 41-43

CHAPTER 3

OPPORTUNITY ENABLERS

"Look, I'm sending you out as sheep among wolves, so be wary and wise as serpents but as harmless as doves, innocent and without pretense. Be wary of men who will betray you, but know this will yield opportunity, so do not be anxious, for your response will be given to you by the Holy Spirit." Matthew 10:16-20

In these few words, Jesus outlined the context, the strategy, the alternatives, the response and the expectation for those heeding the call to make a difference.

Confronting darkness where it counts, at the point of destruction's thrust, will yield opportunity. It is the grand-strategy of Light against darkness. It is the dimension where God's supernatural intervention is the only option. It is the total reliance on faith and Kingdom principles when it is all on the line. It is where the fire falls. It pivots on change.

The Dynamic

Change that matters will not yield to simple idealism; nor will it result from even the best of human achievement. The process, that brings change to a generation, sparks the fire of God. Jesus said everyone would be seasoned with fire (Mark 9). The Gospels also speak of a baptism of fire, in addition to Jesus indicating that he had come to cast fire upon the earth (Luke 12).

Hebrews tells us that God is a consuming fire. The fire of God's presence stops-cold the work, and consumes the entanglements of the enemy. The fire of God is the source to the power that transforms.

Those entrusted with a mantle of change bear a high calling that requires an increasingly deeper penetration into the place of His presence and with that, a walk marked by fire. Those who wield the fire must be prepared to walk through the fire.

The mantle of change is a walk that was patterned by the life of Joseph, who prevailed at each level and at the set-time, executed his assignment with precision. He served to rescue his people from the destruction unleashed to destroy them; and brought about change that bestowed blessing and great benefit to all those under and touched by his authority.

Joseph is a graphic example of the cost and the process required of those yielded to the higher calling that will change a generation and make an impact for eternity. Joseph is the model for mobilizing and dispensing the resources to bring the transformation that harnesses a nation and people, to bring about God's redemptive purposes, while serving as a gatekeeper for opportunity.

Yielding to this higher calling, involves the willingness to face and walk through the fires, as Joseph's prophetic gift and wisdom was tempered, honed and refined to enable a clarity in discerning God's voice in decisions of state. This tempered prophetic gift and wisdom in Joseph was the catalyst to the power to penetrate the lairs of darkness that released sequential turning points that bore on the process that converged to impact eternity.

The Process

Penetrating the heart of darkness, to where opportunity yields, is at the core of this process.

"Look, I'm sending you out as sheep among wolves, so be wary and wise as serpents but as harmless as doves, innocent and without pretense. Be wary of men who will betray you, but know this will yield opportunity, so do not be anxious, for your response will be given to you by the Holy Spirit." Matthew 10:16-20

Jesus made it very clear in this sequence that in serving as His ambassadors, not only would we be vulnerable, we would be sent to where the duty is perilous and risky. The context of sheep among wolves defines the setting. Yet, the Lord makes the strategy clear by comparing the ways of two distinctly different creatures, a serpent and a dove.

The serpent knows when to stay put and be hidden; and when to traverse its territory. When it moves, it does so quickly, skillfully, silently and purposefully. It is wise and strategic. The dove, on the other hand, gives no appearance of being a threat, as it openly, but remotely goes about its everyday activities. It is pure in heart.

Joseph demonstrated his spiritual agility through his service. A key Kingdom principle tied to leadership is that we lead by serving. Before he was sold into slavery, his dreams gave him a glimpse into the significance of his calling. They actuated the faith for him to prevail against adversity. At each level, prior to his promotion to sit alongside of Pharaoh and his entrance into the fullness of his calling, Joseph not only demonstrated faithfulness, but he was recognized as the bearer of God's blessings by those around him. He was wise, strategic and pure in heart.

"The Lord was with Joseph and he was a successful man and everyone saw that the Lord was with Joseph and made all that he did to prosper." Genesis 39: 2, 3

The Snares

For those with the mantle of change, snares can be expected. At the most basic level, snares employ deception. As a slave, the snare for Joseph would have involved him betraying his master. The snare turned out to be double-sided and brought an ugly backlash, with rejection and betrayal. This betrayal was a further mark of Joseph's high calling; a calling which could not be accomplished through his own abilities; but only through God. It accentuated the demonstration of God's power that would be required to yield the release of opportunity in this most unlikely situation. It was a part of the fire tempering Joseph's unique anointing and gifts.

With the examples of the serpent and the dove, Jesus provides insight into the most prevalent snares employed against those serving as His ambassadors of change. For the strategic, it is power and achievement. For the pure in heart, it is idealism.

Achievement. Achievement carries the same potential for being an asset or a snare, for those who are strategic. Achievement carries with it the potential for opportunity, but not without the intoxicating lure of power. Power usurpers abound and short-circuit the intentions of God at the point when change yields opportunity. Jesus said: many are called, but few are chosen. A wide swath of the religious elite of His day misused their positions and callings. It is why Jesus selected and entrusted everyday people to broker the opportunity that would come with His confrontation and defeat of darkness.

Idealism. Idealism is both the strength and the snare for those who are pure in heart. Idealists point the way for change. They create movements. Idealism also can miss the forest for the trees. It has a tendency to throw out the baby with the bathwater. The enemy of our souls wants to snare the pure in heart with an idealism that is so utopian, it is out of touch; with a religious spirit that reflects zeal without knowledge. However, the pure in heart who the enemy can't seem to entice with his distorted form of idealism, become targets of destruction. Yet even with that, they are promoted to serve as catalysts for turning points of opportunity.

Betrayal

Betrayal, by definition, comes from within. It is a false front or disloyalty. Betrayal implies faithless actions from those who should otherwise be trusted or considered on the same team. To betray is to deliver into the hands of the enemy in violation of a trust. Its result destroys, sets back and undermines. Beyond the obvious dangers represented by wolves, there lurk those whose intent and ways demand wariness on our part. They are found among the sheep. They are the betrayers.

Jesus further defined betrayers as *"those who love greetings in the marketplaces, the best seats in the synagogues, the best places at the feasts; who devour widow's houses and for a pretense make long prayers."* While Jesus frequently pointed to the Pharisees and Sadducees, he didn't do so en-mass. The gateway to Jesus' betrayal came from His inner-circle and one who was part of a politically zealous group. It was a band of zealots, whose misguided zeal sought to activate change for God.

Yet, the range of these betrayers all fit under the label Jesus referred to as hypocrites. Hypocrites are pretenders and phonies. They present one face while living another. Despite lip service to the contrary, their quest for power is for their own purposes and gain.

Opportunity

Joseph rightfully tested his brothers. They had betrayed him. In his role of dispensing the grain that would prevent starvation during the prolonged famine, he understood that he was exactly where God wanted him. Nevertheless, he did not need an eruption of unholy fire from ones with their track record, to undermine the significance of his task.

Joseph was wary of his betrayers. Yet, he found his brothers remorseful and so, he took the steps to close the gap and be restored to those he loved most dearly. It not only was Joseph's finest hour, it demonstrated the key dimension accompanying his calling; the generous father's heart of an opportunity enabler.

While Jesus warned us to be wary of and avoid betrayal; He also noted that betrayal would happen. He explained that the backside of betrayal would cause opportunity to yield. This would be the opportunity that operates against the odds. It is opportunity that only God can orchestrate. It is miraculous opportunity that transcends the here and now in its impact.

"Have you entered the treasury of snow or have you seen the storehouse of hail which I have reserved for the time of trouble, for the day of battle and war?" Job 38: 22,23

"For the LORD has opened His armory, and brought out the weapons of His indignation; for this is the work of the Lord God of hosts." Jeremiah 50:25

When betrayal comes, Jesus' word was to be confident in faith and start looking for the opportunity. *The faith-response to betrayal sparks the change whereby opportunity yields.*

Faith and risk go hand in hand. Faith faces the challenges needed to overcome the obstacles in order to seize the opportunities that lie on the backside of the challenges. The greater the challenge; the more significant the opportunity. It's why Jesus said we are blessed when others revile, persecute and make evil statement about us for His sake. (Matthew 5)

The leadership anointing, distinguished by opportunity yielding, is marked by fire. It comes with a cost. It traverses that narrow corridor between life and death. It carries a mantle that spits in the eye of death as it walks through the valley of the shadow of death. It's a pathway where angels converge. (Acts 12)

The Opportunity Enablers

The unique characteristics, of those bearing the mantle of generational change, begin with an authority that challenges the status quo. They operate outside the box. They prevail. They exhibit a maturity that judges righteously, with a father's heart. When change yields, they become the opportunity brokers. Joseph was an opportunity broker. Opportunity brokers are equippers and community-builders. They are enablers and dispensers.

In other words, opportunity enablers operate uniquely to build community; to facilitate, mobilize and equip others. Enablers bear the mark of the highest calling among leaders. They don't build institutions that serve to perpetuate their own existence. Their organizations are outward-driven or integrated into the broader community. They flow with a modus operandi that is consistently serving to extend opportunity to others.

Long ago, there was a pivotal tribe of Israel known as Issachar, who understood the times and knew what to do. They were a comparatively small tribe among the twelve, yet extremely potent in their function. They stood at the point of change, knowing what to do. Within the same context, Jesus admonished us to understand the times and seasons.

The status quo is the enemy of opportunity. Flashpoints of fire will bring change. Change rightly responded to yields opportunity that advances the Kingdom of God.

"The wind goes toward the south and turns around to the north. It whirls about continually and comes again on its circuit." Ecclesiastes 1:6

When evil emerges; faith arises. When the fire falls; opportunity yields. When destiny calls, the enablers arise.

"There is no one who has given up house or brothers or sisters or father or mother or wife or children or lands for My sake and the gospel's who shall not receive a hundredfold now in this age, with persecutions—and in the age to come, eternal life. But many who are first will be last and the last first." Mark 10: 29-31

CHAPTER 4

SPIRITUAL CLUTTER

"Having begun by the Spirit, are you now being perfected by the flesh? So then, does He who provides you with the Spirit and works miracles among you, do it by the works of the Law, or by the hearing with faith?" Galatians 3:3,5

As the times have become more evil, so also the opportunities of God have been increasing. With the increase of opportunities is the need to execute His agendas more strategically. So also is the need for greater spiritual clarity to wisely discern the avenues and spheres for these opportunities.

This spiritual clarity requires a closer look at how we interpret the realities tied to the sovereign initiatives being released by the Lord for this season. The realities for the 21st century Body involves facing the Ephesians 4 premises of maturity and the full knowledge of the Lord, along with the subtleties and snares manifesting against those anointed and called for this hour. Among them are smart people who like their ears tickled with success in ministry carrying a distinctly subtle snare of ambition. The bottom line too often results in what has begun in the Spirit, digressing into the flesh, as we endeavor to accomplish the purposes of God.

The Shift

In the past, it has been nothing short of remarkable what has been gleaned from "glimmers" of God's truth and revelations from His Spirit. Yet, the times call for a transition from the milk to the meat. As the Body moves into maturity, the demands of the times reflect an urgency to penetrate the depths of the Spirit and embrace what the Apostle Paul revealed as the *"full knowledge of the Lord."*

Evil is abounding. With it is a growth in the hostility toward God's people. Standard operating procedures for purposeful Christian agendas are falling short; creating a need to step outside the box spiritually to reevaluate the prisms, the mind-sets and the models by which we go about doing the work of the ministry.

The words Jesus used to announce his earthly ministry: *"The Kingdom of God is at hand"*—have never had greater pertinence. Yet, the Kingdom pathway is, as it was in the days of Jesus, one that is unconventional and goes against the grain.

The Lord sent Joseph ahead into Egypt into paths that defied the accepted traditions and ways of his people. So today God has prepared many who are penetrating and taking their positions in arenas many may consider as unorthodox or even sacrilegious. Business-as-usual in the Church is no longer enough. It is a time of penetrating the fabric of society.

The model requires nothing less than a Kingdom pathway. The old model was driven by a 20th century, western, Anglo-Saxon, Gentile worldview. While this orientation may have served for a time; it is no longer enough and will tend to mislead.

Distorted Realities

There's a TV show titled "Myth Busters." It's a reality-TV science show that has taken on pop-culture myths like: would a penny thrown from the Empire State Building that hit an unwary pedestrian seriously hurt them? (No.) Does a sinking ship suck a passenger on the deck into its downward vortex? (No.) Can you fail a drug test by eating a bagel heavily laden with poppy seeds? (Yes) The show provides a reality check on popularly accepted notions.

A parallel to this premise exists, related to what we as believers embrace spiritually as our operational standards. From generation to generation, we have grown and gained greater clarity to the foundations of our faith we hold dear.

Still for some, those foundations have been doctrinal positions formed decades or longer ago. For others, they are based primarily on personal experience. Some foundations are based on nothing more than a premise found in a hymn, a scene in a movie or passage in a book. Yet, the baseline for our scriptural reality checks is the Word of God. Even then, we filter how we view the realities of God's truth through our own array of cultural and doctrinal prisms. As such, if we are to genuinely understand the times and know what to do, then there are spiritual myths and *"precepts of men,"* along with their "clutter" in need of being challenged, as we seek to advance the Kingdom.

The Balance

The early Church was one of power. It operated in unity. The Gospel of John tells us that they that know Him must know Him in Spirit and in Truth. That means not only rightly dividing the Word of truth, but correctly discerning the voice of the Lord in our roles as His ambassadors. Without that balance, our faith is defective.

Hearing God's voice is what the prophetic is all about. There is a difference between being a prophet and being prophetic. Every born-again believer needs to be developing their prophetic gift—because without an ability to recognize His voice—the balance of our faith between Spirit and Truth is severely hampered and subject to being governed by the arm of the flesh rather than the flow of the Spirit.

The power of God is uniquely connected to hearing the voice of the Lord. Miracles and transformation will never rest on a formula or human effort, but rather on being rightly connected to the Spirit of God and operating in unison with Him.

The Clutter

However, when the enemy can't stop a believer from growing in their discernment of God's voice, his strategy shifts to CLUTTER—diverting and diluting the pure voice of the Lord with the impact of meaningless disorder and confusion. It is the place that a large part of the Body finds itself—plagued with distractions in the face of the enemy mounting an offensive.

The Merriam-Webster Dictionary defines "to clutter" as: *"to fill or cover with things in disorder or scattered at random or with things that impede movement or action or reduce effectiveness."* The noun is defined as: *"a mass of disorderly or distracting objects or details."* The American Heritage Dictionary adds*: "a confused noise" or "to run with confusion."*

Spiritual "clutter" always appeals to the passions rather than the Spirit. Passion without the Spirit will distort truth. "Clutter" typically will include enough elements of the truth to appear valid; yet more often than not will mask the more excellent way. Clutter has the appearance of usefulness because it includes elements that are valid or may once have been valid. Yet, in the final analysis, it serves to mask, to distract and to undermine.

Yet the Body has embraced a repertoire of outdated and wheel-spinning clutter that ranges from our doctrinal mind-sets; almost sacrosanct, outdated ministry operating procedures; an array of eschatological presuppositions; denominational spins on Kingdom priorities; along with political interpretations of the times and the latest conspiracy theories that far too frequently guide our response to issues of societal transformation.

Headstrong Blindness. The concept of Charismatic witchcraft comes from those either blatantly misusing or simply exercising their gifts in a wrong manner—of misfiring because of a headstrong blindness of purpose and perspective. The result of serving the Lord with outmoded mind-sets, prisms and models has been a reckless, self-absorbed orientation, that has resulted in a fractionalized Body with far too many who support their separateness by destructive, self-righteous finger-pointing and flaw-seeking.

Jesus imparted the pivotal truth that for us to be entrusted with the higher levels of advancing this Kingdom that He came to set in motion—that we need to deal with the beams in our own eyes before we can ever begin addressing the splinters in the eyes of others. Misguided zeal and misuses of power will ultimately self-destruct.

Avoiding the Clutter

Avoiding the clutter will be the result when we connect the Hebrew roots to the worldview of our faith; begin maturely discerning the Lord's voice; and proactively embrace a Kingdom perspective.

Avoiding the clutter will involve guarding against the reckless and impetuous actions created by the zeal tied to our initial impressions when hearing the voice of the Lord. Hearing God's voice is a Holy thing; one that must be treated with respect. Avoiding the clutter will involve guarding against the dependencies that create myopic or premature responses rather than giving birth to genuine Kingdom agendas.

Discerning the Voice of the Lord

Clutter is what results when we attempt to connect the dots with that which falls short of God's plan. Clutter results from working out in the flesh what was begun in the Spirit. Clutter manifests when we yield to the constraints of the precepts of men. Clutter happens when we fall short in hearing the full revelation from God's voice.

The prophet Isaiah used the analogy of sheep to describe the people of God who were straying. They strayed because their fear toward Him was based on what they could comfortably grasp—*the precepts of men*—with the result being each one choosing "*his own way.*" It is the subtle distinction between soul and spirit, which is the distinguishing mark between intellectualism and the unrestrained power of God. There is a huge difference between a mobilized Body rightly connected to the heart of God, and those whose primary means of "hearing" the voice of the Lord being the next trendy word coming from whatever source or spin they have learned to depend on.

That's not to suggest that we can't glean from others. What it does suggest relates to the dependency on words from others, rather than on a personal interaction that comes with maturity and accurately discerning God's voice for ourselves. It is an issue that relates to the time we spend with Him.

Principles, Wisdom and Revelation. There are three primary dimensions tied to God's Word that must operate in concert when discerning His voice and giving opportunity for revelation to achieve its full purposes. First are the *principles* of God's Word. These principles are foundational and require maturity in rightly dividing the Word of Truth for a given application.

Second, is the *wisdom* applied to the principles. Wisdom flows with the dynamic of kindness and has no foundation in the zeal tied to worldly ambition. Wisdom is a dimension of the operation of the Spirit and marks the difference between random intellectualism and sound interpretation of Scripture that has Life as its result.

Then, there is the *revelation* of God in which the Spirit prompts, imparts and speaks to an individual. Revelation is never out of context and our response to revelation should always be to return to the presence of the Lord with questions. Those questions need to define the context of the revelation and its purpose, as well as issues tied to timing. This is what is intended when we bathe revelation in prayer. *The **full revelation of God** will always be built upon the principles of God and flow in the wisdom of God.*

In the same way that we have been admonished in Peter's epistles to submit to the washing of the Word, so we must also make it a practice to bathe in prayer, the revelations we receive in His presence.

Revelation, Illumination, Instruction, Direction and Release.
In far too many instances, a believer genuinely receives a revelation—and the first thing that happens is that they shoot into the stratosphere with that revelation, rather than returning to the presence of the Lord to get the illumination on the revelation. Likewise, once the illumination is received, there needs to be still more time spent in the presence of the Lord in order to get the instruction on the illumination. Then, once the instruction is received—we need to inquire of the Lord on the direction and timing on the instruction. Ideally, the sequence includes *a release from the Lord* before putting in action the steps discerned.

The point is that *on strategic issues*, when we hear from the Lord, the revelation needs to be treated with respect and bathed in prayer AND properly birthed, rather than randomly being acted on as if it were magic.

Our Worldview

Our worldview is the collection of beliefs and perceptions through which we interpret life around us. Our worldview forms the basis on which we discern and make decisions on matters concerning our lives.

The scripture says we see in part and we prophesy in part. To an extent, that is because our prisms and models are incomplete. Yet, Ephesians 4 points to a time of coming into the full knowledge of the Lord. While some interpret that as perfecting our doctrine, in reality it is the restoration of the operational equation for which God created man in the first place.

Genesis 2 speaks of man being created to rule over the work of God's hands with God and Adam walking and talking in the cool of the evening. God's purpose for man was a cooperative management process. The full knowledge of the Lord referred to by Paul is not a doctrine, but a cooperative means of operating in concert through the Body, in our efforts to accomplish the purposes and will of God. Over the years, man has progressively left God out of the equation. Even in the church, we've relegated Him to a back-seat position when we pray along the lines of: *"here's my plan Lord, now please bless it!"*

Restoring this vital, interactive process calls for a revamping of our worldview. The worldview the Lord set up from the beginning involved a merging of the economic, community and spiritual. These foundations have their basis in a Hebrew worldview. When the Apostle Paul wrote the churches about the *"riches of His glory,"* his worldview was not a 20th century, Gentile worldview. Paul was a rabbi, a Jewish teacher of the Torah. So, when he spoke of the riches of God's glory, it included not just the spiritual riches, but the ones that were a part of the Jewish roots and heritage of the Word: the community and economic dimensions.

Somehow the economic and community riches of God's glory have fallen into the separation-of-church-and-state worldview— with the church accepting them as something only to be pursued through human effort. The "new thing" underway will impact both the mind-sets and models by which we have approached the work of the ministry in recent years. Together, hearing His voice and our worldview, bear on the restoration of God's Kingdom rule.

Embracing the Kingdom Perspective

Operating according to the principles of the Kingdom is the threshold Jesus outlined that leads into the supernatural. It is the arena where Spirit controls matter. It is the realm of faith where the unseen is the substance behind that which is seen.

Jesus' message of the Kingdom of God broke the mold of the religious "organization man" of His day—and ours. What He outlined left no place for phonies, opportunists or zealots. Operating according to the principles of God's Kingdom is the dividing-asunder that distinguishes our human effort from steps needed in a cooperative effort initiated and directed by God. It is the place beyond our human effort where ambition falls short of God's purposes because it goes against the grain of Kingdom principles.

Kingdom principles involve the choice to participate in His plan or to pursue our own desires. It is the choice to operate according to His principles or to work it out our own way. Advancing the Kingdom of God means we need to embrace His principles, wisdom and revelation. God is always at the center in the operation of his Kingdom.

Operating in God's Kingdom begins with the principle of dominion. Authority, faith and dominion go hand in hand. Dominion involves the creative process required to subdue the earth. It is the basis of God's charge to us to cooperatively *rule over the work of his hands*. Dominion is the foundation of Kingdom rule and the principle of increase. It is foundational to entrepreneurship. Deuteronomy 28:13 tells us that *"The Lord is making you the head and not the tail and you will always mount higher and not decline."* Together with faith; stewardship and diligence enter the Kingdom equation to create the Kingdom principle of multiplication. Perseverance and unity likewise are foundational to the establishment of plans and the way we operate with others in this process of *"ruling over the work of His hands."*

Jesus explained what had been as a mystery to so many for so long in these principles of God's Kingdom. They often seem contradictory to what we consider as the natural order of doing things. We advance by yielding. Leadership comes from serving. Honor comes through humility. Wisdom is found in simplicity. We extend charity to our enemies. Our purpose in life comes through giving it up. Perfect love eliminates fear. We receive when giving. In our weakness we are made strong. Ownership increases by sharing.

Jesus didn't come to establish a "new" order of things. He came to restore what God intended from the time when God and Adam walked and talked in the cool of the evening and discussed the matters God had assigned Adam. Jesus came to remove the clutter and to reorder our purpose to what it was from the beginning.

The Convergence and Overcoming: Entering God's Rest

Entering God's rest or Shabbat, as outlined in the book of Hebrews is the pivot point and catalyst to hearing His voice, adjusting our worldview and embracing a Kingdom perspective. It is the place where we cease striving and human effort gives way to the ongoing flow of the Spirit. It is the place where the supernatural and the extraordinary become the normal way of life.

The rest of God, God's Shabbat is just not a once a week affair. It incorporates the need for a shift from our 20th century, western, Gentile worldview to be able to fully embrace its significance. Much like the "charity of God" as it was translated in 1 Corinthians 13 in the King James version, it reflects dynamics tied to the Hebraic roots of our faith.

From the time of creation, the Lord knew man needed a time to recalibrate and realign. God's rest preceded the Ten Commandments (Genesis 2:3 and Exodus 16:4, 28-30). It brings refreshment and a reinvigoration of our God-ordained creative energies and is a time set-aside to give special focus and honor to the Lord. It reflects the model of how we need to pace ourselves and integrate all we do *in cooperation with Him*. God's rest also involves an element of protection and the fulfillment of God's promises. (Isaiah 58:13 and Jeremiah 17:19) It will be observed in the new earth (Isaiah 66:23). The Word also promises blessings to the non-Jewish "foreigner" who keeps the Sabbath (Isaiah 56: 1-8). God's rest, while outlined in the commandments, is not so much an obligation as it is a gateway into the refreshing and blessings of God.

In our zeal and tendency toward *making-do* out of the glimmers of our revelations and worldviews, we have surrounded ourselves with CLUTTER. The times are evil and demand more. The clutter needs to be identified and bypassed. The devil is coming out of the closet. The gloves have been removed. The pathways of the past are no longer enough. There is an urgency tied to the times we have entered, that require MORE, much more, than what has been needed in the past.

Spirit and Truth are the cornerstones to our walk with the Lord. Dominion, faith and authority provide the gateway into the arena of our God-intended purpose. The mix of maturely discerning the voice of the Lord; embracing a realistic biblical worldview; and the operation of God's Kingdom principles converge with entering His rest, to lay an axe to the root of selfish ambition, fear, rebellion, manipulation, rejection and the whole array of soul issues that plague an otherwise active and well-intentioned Church.

The word to the Church for this hour is to "*come up here, above the clutter.*" The time of crossing over to living beyond our passions, traditions and clutter—and entering the domain where God reigns, is upon us. The choice is both the challenge and the pathway.

"*For creation itself longs for the revealing of the sons of God that it might be delivered from the bondage of corruption as it gains entrance into this glorious freedom. For we know that all creation groans and labors with birth pangs together until now.*" Romans 8:19-22 "*So Jesus said: The Son can do nothing by himself, he can do only what he sees his Father doing because whatever the Father does the Son also does. For the Father loves the Son and shows him all that he does. To your amazement he will show you greater things than these*". John 5:19,20 "*I am the vine; you are the branches. Whoever abides in me and I in him, he will bear much fruit; apart from me you can do nothing. If you abide in me and my words abide in you, ask whatever you wish, and it will be given you.*" John 15:5,7

CHAPTER 5

DISCERNING THE KINGDOM

"The Son of Man will send out His angels, and they will gather out of His kingdom all things that offend, and those who practice lawlessness, and will cast them into the furnace of fire. Then the righteous will shine forth as the sun in the kingdom of their Father."
Matthew 13: 41-43

Within the Kingdom is the practice of lawlessness, those who abuse the power, authority and gifts of God.

After a time of using parables to teach the crowds about the Kingdom of God, Jesus pulled away with His disciples. In explaining the parable of the tares to them, He pointed out that within His Kingdom would be found those who have been planted by the evil one. They are the ones recognized by the practice of lawlessness, while the true sons of the Kingdom are described as "the righteous."

The context takes place in the approach to the end of the age. What Jesus is saying in Matthew 13 is that within the Kingdom are "things that offend" and the practice of lawlessness which darken the impact of the true sons of the Kingdom. Once the angels remove the lawless-plants, the righteous will shine with the brightness of the sun.

The signs of the times suggest greater clarity to our functional grasp of God's Kingdom and with that, a closer look into our understanding of lawlessness and "the righteous."

Lawlessness

The practice of lawlessness in the Kingdom stems from those who abuse and misuse the power, authority and gifts of God. Not to be confused with the sin and disorder in the world, Kingdom lawlessness serves to compromise, divert and usurp the will of God. It is driven by a "self" orientation, rather than the community-good whereby God's people are blessed to be a blessing. It confuses the strategic with short-term fixes.

Jesus made the basis of Kingdom lawlessness very plain as He described the significance of being aligned with God's will.

"Not every one who says to Me, 'Lord, Lord,' will enter the Kingdom of Heaven, but he who does the will of my Father. Many will come to Me and say, 'Lord have we not prophesied in Your name, cast out demons and done many wonders?' I will declare them, 'I never knew you, depart from Me, you who practice lawlessness.'" Matthew 7:21

Within the book of Revelation are examples of those within the Church who practice forms of lawlessness ranging from sowing stumbling blocks to undermining the work of the Spirit with agendas that seduce, hinder, confuse and undermine. It speaks of those who ascribe positions of spiritual authority to themselves that are false and not in keeping with the work of the Spirit.

Faith and Humility

Presumption tied to a vision or a gift will undermine an otherwise valid call of God. Faith without humility will ultimately deceive and corrupt. It has never been what we can do for God, but rather what we allow Him to do through us. Even Jesus noted that: *"He could do nothing of Himself, He could only do what He saw the Father doing."* Our dependency can never be on anything other than operating in oneness with the Lord, in both Spirit and Truth.

While the central theme of Jesus' teaching was on the principles and pathways of the Kingdom, Judas embraced a distorted view of the Kingdom. He missed the main point. Jesus taught that to truly enter the Kingdom of Heaven, we must become as little children. Children bow to proper authority with joy. With zeal and expectation, they go about fulfilling their purpose.

Joseph was a prime example of the balance between faith and humility. Despite being alone and in the most adverse of circumstances, his righteousness shined brightly and was recognized by all those around him while he was yet a slave and then when he was in prison. His faithfulness and stewardship enabled him to become a father to Pharaoh and be given the authority over the resources needed to avert the destruction colliding with the world at that time.

The Righteous and Stewardship

Jesus came to set things in order, to close the gap in the change needed to reset the default button in a world run amok. That's why, again and again, He announced His earthly ministry with the words: *"the Kingdom of God is at hand."* He denounced the false righteousness of the religious elite and pointed to true Kingdom righteousness.

"So I say to you that tax collectors and harlots will enter the kingdom of God before you. The kingdom of God will be taken from you and given to a people bearing its fruits." Matt 21:31, 43

Jesus instructed his followers to be wary of the false, the phonies and the counterfeits with the wisdom that we would *"know them by their fruits."* Righteousness, as God intended it, is foundational to the Kingdom. For Kingdom righteousness to manifest, it must be entwined with stewardship.

Roughly half the scriptures on righteousness are in the context of stewardship. The parable of the talents alone makes a strong case for this point. Still there is much more to this truth in both the New and Old Covenants. The Jewish Torah is filled with examples and principles that bear on the combined spiritual, community and entrepreneurial stewardship-dynamic by which the righteous are to bring hope and restoration to a world in darkness.

Yet the inclination of God's people to separate and retreat into monastic-type communities has been evidenced throughout both Jewish and Christian history. Jesus trained His followers and then sent them out — into the world. Our job, in the face of overwhelming odds of adversity, is to bring change to society.

"Your Kingdom come, Your will be done on earth, as it is in heaven." Matt 6:10

The title of a book I recently came across provides great insight into understanding the Kingdom-focus in the strategy Jesus was imparting and releasing. It is a history of the Jewish people who settled Colorado during the mid-1800s. Its title is *"Pioneers, Peddlers and 'Tzadikim."*

Over the centuries God's people, Jew and Gentile alike have been called as pioneers, to bring change that benefits society around them. That goal cannot be harnessed without the entrepreneurial, which is the ability to bring increase and blessing by identifying opportunity and doing something about it, while serving genuine needs of the community. However, the issue is more than just capitalizing on opportunity. It is intrinsically linked with stewardship. It is bringing increase by serving with a Kingdom purpose in mind.

The Pathway of the Righteous

Bringing change that bears God's blessing will not be accomplished without the involvement of God's Hand and a God-centered identity. Such is the identity of the 'Tzadikim. 'Tzadikim is the Hebrew word for "the righteous" among God's people. The righteous are sent forth to shine in the midst of a world of darkness and confusion. 'Tzadikim is a recognized identity that is ascribed to an individual by those around them.

But there's more to this Hebrew word. "Tz'dakah—righteousness" also means charity, the type of charity that builds community. It was to the 'Tzadikim—righteous that it was said, *"Inasmuch as you've done it to the least of these my brethren, you've done it unto me."* (Matt 25:40) So, the righteousness of the 'Tzadikim points not to position or some self-serving, self-contained piety, but rather to ones who are a light paving the way and benefiting the communities of their spheres in a way that advances God's Kingdom.

"Nations will come to your light, and kings to the brightness of your rising." Isaiah 60:3

God's hand upon the Jewish people is evidenced by the impact Jews have made on the world. Jews gave birth to Western civilization. Our most treasured values have evolved from Jewish beliefs. From the Torah have come the foundational principles of the world's most successful governmental, legal, moral and economic systems.

Joseph is counted among the 'Tzadikim. He was sent to shine, to bring blessing and change in Egypt. In Genesis 39, the scripture says that *"everyone saw that the Lord was with Joseph and made all that he did to prosper."* That observation was made when he was a slave in Potiphar's house. Those practicing sorcery and idolatry observed it. Joseph was blessed to be a blessing and the world around him recognized God's goodness through him.

Yet, there is a reality Jesus points to regarding the tares among the wheat, for us to understand the "righteous" within the Kingdom. It bears on the *"things that offend"* and those who carry the identity of God; who, despite their personal intentions, are in reality practicing lawlessness.

"Why are you so foolish? Having begun by the Spirit, are you now being perfected by the flesh? So then, does He who provides you with the Spirit and works miracles among you, do it by the works of the Law, or by the hearing with faith?" Galatians 3:3,5

The issue begins with the balance between Spirit and Truth. While the foundation will always be based on the principles of God's Word, the supernatural is based on our obedient response to His voice as we flow in the Spirit. When that balance is combined with faithful stewardship, then just as was the case for Joseph at each stage in his tenure in Egypt, a transfer of the world's authority being served will become the basis for change and the recognition of God's role in the situation.

Discerning the Kingdom

God's Kingdom is where God's authority rules. While it begins in our hearts, it extends to the sphere of influence in which we are entrusted. It is the power and authority that confronts darkness, reverses the curse and brings change to society. The Kingdom of God is the source of Life that holds the hope and future sought by the people of the world.

"The Kingdom of God is not a matter of talk, but of power." 1 Corinthians 4:20

The calling of Joseph was about a realignment needed to bring forth a genuine advancement of God's Kingdom rule. So it is today. The Joseph-calling is not a Christian-enterprise self-improvement program, nor is it a pathway or model for success as the world views success. Neither is it a Christian benevolence program.

The Joseph-calling is the establishment of *influence* that, through the authority of God, reverses the bondage of corruption and releases societal transformation. Its pathway involves entrance *"within the veil"* for which Jesus was a forerunner. It is reserved for the righteous who will shine forth as the sun in the Kingdom of the Father.

It is the recognition of that Kingdom authority that becomes the basis of the trust-response that results in the true Josephs being granted the authority of their Pharaohs. Without the operation of the Joseph-Pharaoh alliance, the Joseph-calling is premature and incomplete.

So it is that we've entered a time for those poised with this calling to be alert to the shift in events released only by the Father's authority. It's a time to be wary of being seduced by the tares and the things that offend. It is a time to be about His business. It is a time in which the righteous will be released into their spheres to shine forth as the sun. There's a cost to the calling. Yet, for those who prevail, the joy will overshadow the demands of the birthing.

"Now salvation, and the power and the kingdom of our God and the authority of His Christ have come, for the accuser of the brethren has been thrown down." Revelation 12:10

CHAPTER 6

THE MATURITY MANTLE

"Let the words of my mouth and the meditations of my heart be acceptable in your sight, O Lord." Psalm 19:4

One of the most serious stumbling blocks to the Body maturity spoken of in Ephesians is the words of our mouths and the meditations, or attitudes of our hearts. The issue has little bearing on achieving model character. Nor is it a conformity thing. It is foremost a heart issue that pivots on the depth of our relational connection with the Lord. It is also a corporate calling issue.

We all yearn for an outpouring of His power. We cry out for more of Him. We pray for a new move of God. Yet, within the Body are destructive undercurrents that undermine both His power and Body maturity. These are undercurrents driven by the amassing of loose, misguided tongues.

While there are a range of sources for these lethal undercurrents, including corporate witchcraft schemes, the deadliest have as their source ones anointed for service, whose callings have fallen short of operating in His rest.

The Apostle Paul discerned and incisively laid an axe to the root of sorcery-based undercurrents impeding an initiative he was pursuing.

"Then Saul, filled with the Holy Spirit, looked intently at the sorcerer and said, 'You who are full of all deceit and all fraud, you

son of the devil, you enemy of all righteousness, will you not cease perverting the straight ways of the Lord? And now, indeed, the hand of the Lord is upon you, and you shall be blind, not seeing for a time.'" Acts 13:6

Yet sadly, undermining influences far too often come from within our ranks. The Lord's sovereign intervention with Shebna is a sober warning to those who misdirect the trust expected in their oversight of God's people.

"To Shebna, I will throw you away violently and there you will die. Then it shall be in that day, that I will call My servant Eliakim. I will clothe him with your robe and strengthen him with your belt; I will commit your responsibility into his hand. He shall be a father to the inhabitants of Jerusalem and to the house of Judah. The key of the house of David I will lay on his shoulder; so he shall open, and no one shall shut; and he shall shut, and no one shall open. I will fasten him as a peg in a secure place, and he will become a glorious throne to his father's house. They will hang on him all the glory of his father's house." Isaiah 22:15-23

The Gravity of Destructive Undercurrents

The amassing and intertwining of destructive undercurrents from those anointed for service counter the fervent, effectual prayers of the righteous and short-circuit critical timing issues, along with obstructing the full knowledge of the Lord. It reflects a fine line between righteous and necessary judgment on the one hand and the unrighteous and misguided wielding of power on the other.

Either the cycle of snares tied to these undercurrents must be broken or we will enter a time of cleansing from-on-high that cuts it short. To a large extent, it is a maturity issue that pivots on the cost paid for the corporate calling.

The Cost of the Corporate Calling

There is no calling or ministry that yields genuine transformation, without paying the cost. The cost is tied to risk. Risk is tied to laying it all on the line, with no conditions to following Him. As Jesus said, *"Many are called, but few are chosen."*

Beyond our individual responses to the Lord, there comes a time when we are corporately called to account. Addressing the churches in Revelation, the Spirit of the Lord outlined a balance of expectations to His priorities. This past generation in the West has ridden the momentum of a unique and powerful surge of revival that dates back to the sixties. The result has been acceleration toward spiritual and church growth. Yet, for all the trappings of achievement, as a church, the West has largely fallen short on the issue of the cost.

Whether it is the loss of the first love, or works that fall short, or the trap of being lukewarm; there is a leadership void of strategically shepherding the Body into the maturity required to regain the momentum yearned for by the Spirit.

A major part of the Body outside the West lives under persecution for their faith. We refer to it as the suffering church. Yet, unconsciously we seem to conclude that as the successful, Western expression of the Body, that our pathway represents the model for others. Yet, in the words marking the calling of Paul, one whose impact molded the first-century church, we get a glimmer of the cost of the calling.

"I will show him the many things that he must suffer for my sake." Acts 9:16

For the suffering church, becoming a believer can and often does result in the loss of freedoms ranging from one's standing in the community, to one's job, to the simple liberty of coming and going ...with many who have paid the ultimate sacrifice for their faith.

"For this reason the wisdom of God said, 'I will send them prophets and apostles, of whom they will persecute and put to death, that the blood of all the prophets, which was shed from the foundation of the world, may be required of this generation.'" Lk 11:49, 50

The entrance is through the narrow gate. Disillusionment results when those seeking to enter the narrow gate, are confronted with the ambition and self-serving success mantras of those who force their way to the forefront without the heart to genuinely serve. There's a world seeking the reality of the Lord operating in our midst, not those whose intellectual and institutional facades conform to the world around them. It pivots on the cost.

"In your struggle against sin, you have not yet resisted to the point of shedding your own blood." Hebrews 12:4

Understanding the Times and the Issues

The time at hand bears a critical significance. The global amassing of evil requires nothing less than a mature, mobilized Body, willing to pay the cost. There is an urgent need to remove the undercurrents; the strongholds flowing from misguided tongues and attitudes of those anointed for service; who are striving for the wrong reasons.

Unless judgment is self-initiated, the Spirit of the Lord is going to rid Himself of the destructive stumbling blocks coming from those holding back Body maturity for their own gain. The fire has already begun falling.

"Their idols speak deceit, the diviners see visions that lie; they tell false dreams and give comfort in vain. So the people wander like sheep oppressed for lack of a shepherd." Zech 10:2

The Snares to Corporate Maturity

The major snares fueling these undercurrents include pride, the approval of men, deceit and selfish ambition.

Pride. There is no level of pride more subtle or deadly than spiritual pride. Being used by God carries a higher standard, along with the requirement of regular, effectual time alone in His presence. It involves a regular washing of oneself in the Word, an ongoing emptying of self and a heart of humility that yearns to advance the Kingdom by serving as an opportunity enabler.

"Behold the proud. He enlarges his desires as hell. He is like death and cannot be satisfied. Because you have plundered many nations, the remnant of the people shall plunder you! Woe to him who covets evil gain for his house; to set his nest on high; to be delivered from the power of disaster. Giving shameful counsel in his own house; sinning against his own soul. Woe to him who builds with bloodshed and establishes with iniquity. For the earth will be filled with the knowledge of the glory of God!" Hab 2:4-13

Approval of Men. Proverbs reflects a series of scriptures on the value of wise counsel. The subtle snare among ministry leaders is in surrounding themselves with "yes-men." This is not to suggest the companionship of a contingent of "Job's friends." However, the balance is in seeking out those with sufficient experience and maturity to speak the truth in love.

"Beware of those who love greetings in the marketplaces, the best seats in the synagogues, and the best places at feasts, who devour widows' houses, and for a pretense make long prayers." Mark 12: 38-40

Deceit. On the most basic level, deceit is a misrepresentation or false front. It takes courage to be real. It begins in our prayer closets, with the admonition *"to speak truth in our own hearts,"* as described in Psalm 15. On a higher level, deceit runs rampant when manipulation, rather than love and wisdom, is the means by which leadership is exercised.

"'Through deceit they refuse to know Me, says the LORD. 'Behold, I will refine them and try them. Their tongue is an arrow shot out; it speaks deceit; they speak peaceably to their neighbor with their mouth, but in their heart they lie in wait. Shall I not punish them for these things? Shall I not avenge Myself on such a people as this?'" Jer 9:6-9

Selfish Ambition. Kingdom leadership involves service. The higher the calling, the greater the cost. The mask, that confuses the wisdom and direction needed to serve at higher levels with personal ambition, must be stripped and continually checked. Jesus clearly explained this truth in Luke 5: 6,7 when He said: *"Unto him that much is given, much is required; and to whom men have committed much, of him they will ask the more."* He also punctuated this point with: *"Gentile rulers lord over them and their great ones wield their authority. Not so with you. Let him who is the greatest become the least, and the leader as the servant."* Luke 22: 25-27

The Mantle for Maturity

This is a time for the passing of the mantle between generations. It is a mantle serving to release corporate maturity. For those called to leadership, paying the cost is not an option. The path is narrow and difficult; yet the impact beyond natural expectations and abilities. Entering His rest with Kingdom principles will beam the light required to traverse this pathway. In the words of Jesus:

"He who loves his life will lose it, but he who hates his life in this world will gain it for eternal life." John 12:24-25

One of the greatest clues to leaders who fall short in operating in His rest within local congregations is when the focus gives anything less than first priority to *"perfecting of the saints for the work of the ministry."* This serious breach, aggravated by misguided ministry gatekeepers, becomes the seedbed for undercurrents. Zealots, who will stop at nothing to protect "their ministry," withhold opportunity from others, with precedence given their own ambition as they use others to achieve their self-appointed goals.

This dynamic perpetuates, instead of closing the unscriptural void, between the clergy and the laity within church settings. It sows seeds of destruction and division among those who otherwise would serve as collaborators. It is a misuse of power. When accompanied by whispers, words, attitudes, actions ...and far too often misdirected "prayers," those guilty of this modus operandi won't hesitate to climb over the backs of others for their own selfish ambitions.

Closing the Gap

Closing the gap to corporate maturity will happen only when leaders, from across the globe, recognize and embrace the cost of the calling and enter His rest. It will involve regular times of seeking the Lord, as they check their own ambitions against the priorities outlined for the Churches in Revelations. It will involve a commitment willing to laying it all on the line.

The Least of These. The litmus test for the pathway to corporate maturity is the response to *"the least of these our brethren."*

"Whoever causes one of these little ones who believe in me to stumble, it would be better if a millstone were hung around his neck and he were cast into the sea." Mark 9: 40-42

Opportunity Enabling. A genuine Kingdom perspective reflects a wisdom and zeal that facilitates and nurtures God's calling for others. True greatness and corporate maturity will follow in the wake of those who open doors and enable Kingdom opportunity for others. Jesus' words further enlighten us: *"He who speaks from himself seeks his own glory; but He who seeks the glory of the One who sent Him is true, and no unrighteousness is in Him."* John 7:18-19

The foundation to maturity, as well as to ministry-that-endures is found in the paradoxical Kingdom dynamics imparted to us by Jesus. We extend love to our enemies. Ownership increases by sharing. True leadership is the result of serving. Honor comes through humility. Wisdom is found in simplicity. Making your assets multiply will bring promotion. Growth comes by giving to others. We move forward by yielding. Our purpose in life comes through giving it up. Perfect love eliminates fear. In our weakness God's strength is manifested. We bless those who curse us. We receive when giving.

The Apostle Paul wrote about a time in which those from the very elect would be deceived. Let us prayerfully heed his warning and be alert for the subtleties of the snares, with our lamps trimmed, as we corporately make the choices to pay the cost to be about His business. The need is for servant leaders, who enable opportunity for others. The need is to mobilize, equip and to send.

"We proclaim Him, admonishing and teaching each one with all wisdom, so that we may present every man perfect in Christ. To this end I labor, striving according to His power, which mightily works within me." Col 1:28-29

It is a time to cast our crowns before Him. It is a time to go beyond the lip service of laying down our lives …with a genuine laying down of our ambitions. It is a time to yield to the cost required for those who will emerge as the leaders for a generation that will bring the Body into maturity.

"For everyone will be seasoned with fire, and every sacrifice will be seasoned with salt. Salt is good, but if the salt loses its flavor, how will you season it? Have salt in yourselves and peace with one another." Mark 9: 49-50

CHAPTER 7

THE COST OF THE PATHWAY

"Then the wrath of Elihu was aroused against Job because he justified himself rather than God. Also against his three friends his wrath was aroused, because they had found no answer, and yet had condemned Job." Job 32:2-3

The story of Job provides one of the oldest and richest insights into the realities that bridge the spiritual and the natural; of a foundational dynamic that links God and the righteous, along with the dichotomy between the religious and righteous.

Job was described by God as blameless and upright, a man who feared God and shuned evil. Job was a righteous man. He was a Tzadik who represented God as a blessing to his community. Yet Satan's challenge targeted another dimension.

The challenge was that without the blessings of God, Job would blame God for his misfortunes. Upon losing his children, his fortune and his health; despite the prodding of his wife to curse God and die, Job vindicated God's trust in him with the familiar words:

"'The LORD gave and the LORD has taken away. Blessed be the name of the LORD.' Through all this Job did not sin nor did he blame God." Job 1:21-22

Following the tragedies unleashed against Job was the arrival of Job's three friends. Their outward intentions of bringing Job comfort, soon gave way to unfettered charges that his former blessings had been built on weak and shifting sands. In short, they aligned themselves with the destruction arrayed against Job, taking positions as his accusers.

In his misery, Job expressed a heart-cry for hope (Job 6:11). He pondered if success had left him altogether. As his friends prodded, he questioned what he had left. The arrival of Elihu became the spark of a deeper revelation the Lord gave Job. It was a rich glimpse into God's honor and majesty. It brought a perspective that has marked the heroes of faith throughout the centuries.

The Role of Honor

The perspective yielded from the story of Job unveils a compelling truth concerning the importance the Lord ascribes to the honor of the righteous and how that is tied to His honor.

The ease with which Job's friends digressed into becoming his accusers begs the question of an undercurrent that already existed among them; an undercurrent that perhaps was the catalyst that fueled Satan's charge against Job. What was missed in the speculations of Job's friends was the honor the Lord ascribes to the righteous. The increase of the intensity of their rant was well described by Elihu's response:

"His anger burned against his three friends because they had found no answer, and yet had condemned Job." Job 32:3

The reality was that God had Job poised for promotion. That promotion would take him down a pathway that brought clarity to the role of honor. It not only vastly broadened Job's grasp of the Lord's honor and majesty; but it also redefined the foundational honor attributed to the righteous, which Job's friends, for all their words, missed altogether.

"And the LORD said to Eliphaz the Temanite, "My wrath is kindled against you and against your two friends, because you have not spoken of Me what is right as My servant Job has." Job 42:7

The Dynamic

From the time that Cain killed Able, each generation has experienced the reactions of the religious to the righteous. Job was slandered. Noah was mocked. There was a reason God told Abraham to leave his family, his country and his father's house. Joseph's brothers conspired to kill him and at the last moment got rid of him by selling him into slavery. David's presence was both a comfort and torment to Saul, until he purposed to kill David.

Without the aura of success that Job once had, the undercurrent among his friends manifested. It is the difference in response to the superficial and the real. It is the crux of the dichotomy between the religious and the righteous. It is the dividing asunder between Churchianity and the Kingdom.

Jesus pointed to the root of the problem: *"The kingdom of heaven is like a man who sowed good seed in his field; but while his men slept, his enemy came and sowed tares among the wheat and went his way."* Matthew 13:24-26 *"The kingdom of heaven is like a net cast into the sea that gathered some of every kind. When it was full, they sat down and gathered together the good, but threw the bad away."* Matthew 13:47-49

Yet, Jesus pointed out that for those who would be his followers: *"I will give you the keys of the kingdom of heaven, and whatever you bind on earth will be bound in heaven, and whatever you loose on earth will be loosed in heaven."* Matthew 16:19

The blending between the religious and the righteous gives rise to the ambitions and competition of the religious, the manifestations of which range from slander to the outright destruction and removal of the righteous. The ones given the keys to unlocking the Kingdom become targets. Yet the keys they have for advancing the Kingdom are what give them the edge and an immunity from the intentions of the ambitiously religious.

Honor against Overwhelming Odds

Years ago, as the head of a small consulting operation, I published an advertisement to a host of Fortune 500 companies we sought to do business with. The ad showed a graphic of David with a determined grin as he popped the rock into his sling under the shadow of Goliath. The ad positioned our company against some of the largest and best-known consulting firms in the world. Even today, this ad differentiates the ministry and impact we steward.

The truth in this ad gives focus to the perspective held by Job's friends. They banked on outward appearances: on Job's position and success, while overlooking the honor, substance and role tied to the righteous. The role of the righteous may or may not carry the image of success as the world views success.

Upholding God's Honor

The foundational dynamic linking God and the righteous is honor. Honor distinguishes the righteous 'Tzadikim from the religiously ambitious.

The role of the righteous as His ambassadors, within their spheres in word and deed, upholds and points to the honor of God. When the righteous uphold God's honor, the positioning becomes a precursor to the cloak of honor worn only by the righteous.

"I say to you, unless a grain of wheat falls into the ground and dies, it remains alone; but if it dies, it produces much fruit. He who loves his life will lose it, and he who hates his life in this world will keep it for eternal life." John 12:24-25

Honor in the Midst of Your Enemies

When God's honor is upheld and the honor of the righteous 'Tzadikim is given genuine support by the community, then the expectation will be for the community to experience the positive ripples from this dynamic.

"And the LORD gave the people favor in the sight of the Egyptians, as the man Moses was very great in the land of Egypt, in the sight of Pharaoh's servants and in the sight of the people." Exodus 11:3

The book of Acts tells of when: *"Great fear fell upon the church and upon ALL who heard these things."* This was a day in which the dynamic of God's honor was upheld. Stephen was stoned for it. Their leadership was limited to the righteous. God's people were not trying to be like everyone else. Their identity and worldview was fully in God. The righteous 'Tzadikim of the early church were not dealing the success cards mete for church growth; but rather the change tied to building the Kingdom.

Understanding the Times

We've entered a new season. Globally, we are experiencing a shift that penetrates the economic, cultural and political realities governing the course of future events. The stakes are higher, as are the parameters for operating according to God's Kingdom rule. We have to be viewing the realities from God's perspective and ensuring our pathways and models provide anticipatory responses to the changes.

The gap between the two-thirds of the world with little to no middle class and the West is closing. God's righteous ambassadors have always been "out-of-the-box" from the standpoint of the world and the position of the religious. We have not been wired to be like everyone else.

Within the shift underway will be surprises; unveiling unlikely candidates for the tasks of the Kingdom. Ambassadors are emerging from among the suffering and persecuted who may now be as Jobs, poised on their ash heaps, listening to the rants of their unafflicted "friends" coming from their stances of success.

The Cost of the Pathway

True honor follows humility. The revelation Job had came through a pathway of humility and led to the honor only bestowed by God.

"Therefore whoever humbles himself as this little child is the greatest in the kingdom of heaven." Matthew 18:3-5

True humility is the revelation that *"His strength is made perfect in our weakness."* (2 Corinthians 12:8-9) The honor that comes from God has its context in the impact made in community. The price of community leadership is the sacrifice seen in genuine friendship. Jesus described it in John 15:13 when He said: *"Greater love has no one than to lay down his life for his friends."*

God's authentic ambassadors, the ones who sow good seed, the 'Tzadikim, are givers of life. They extend opportunity. When they see the gaps, they work toward filling it in, rather than pointing it out. God is looking for those who will sow the good seeds and pay the cost to avert disasters and build community.

"I sought a man among them who would build up the wall and stand in the gap before Me." Ezekiel 22:30

With their many words, Job's friends had dishonored him. They added to the weight of the burden rather than shouldering it with

Job. They were gap finders, rather than gap-standers. They judged Job with an unbalanced scale based on the limitations of their own perspectives.

*"I say to you that **for every idle word** men may speak, they will give account of it in the day of judgment. For by your words you will be justified, and by your words you will be condemned."* Matthew 12:36-37

The scripture says that Job's friends had no answer and still by their words they condemned Job. In their limited, self-righteous perspectives, they brought God's anger on themselves. Yet, in graciously praying for his friends as he beheld God's honor, Job was promoted into an entire new season of being blessed to be a blessing.

"The LORD restored the fortunes of Job when he prayed for his friends, and the LORD increased all that Job had twofold." Job 42:10-11

SECTION II:

ADDRESSING THE REALITIES

CHAPTER 8

THE SNARE IN SUCCESS

"For rebellion is as the sin of witchcraft, and stubbornness is as idolatry and teraphim (household good luck images). Because you have rejected the word of the Lord, He also has rejected you from being king." 1 Samuel 15:23 Amplified

Two men, David and Saul, both chosen and anointed as king of Israel, had radically different outcomes. Likewise, Judas, chosen to be part of Jesus' inner circle, was seduced by the same deficiencies as Saul.

David committed murder and adultery. Saul's stumbling was over watering down his implementation of the Word of the Lord. Yet David was forgiven and restored, while Saul lost his anointing and position.

Saul's sin incorporated presumption, operating outside the sphere of his authority, an outlook clouded by how he looked to others, and foolish decisions. Despite beginning his tenure as king by prophesying, his downfall was graphically described as rebellion tied to the sin of witchcraft and stubbornness akin to idolatry and the use of good luck charms.

These were incredible men. Each had incredible callings on their lives. Both David's and Saul's downfalls followed what might be considered a time of success. Yet, there were distinct differences bearing on one being restored and the other removed.

Saul got antsy in waiting for Samuel in 1 Samuel 13 and stepped outside his sphere. In 1 Samuel 14, in the battle with the Philistines, Saul was out of touch in an overwhelming situation and drove his people needlessly, while his son Jonathan honored the Lord in the way he redeemed the day for Israel. Both situations held the opportunity to inquire of the Lord. Yet, Saul failed to do so.

Finally, in the battle with the Amalekites in 1 Samuel 15, Saul presumed and compromised what the Word of the Lord had tasked him to do. It was this instance in which Samuel summed up Saul's shortfall as a rebellion that immobilized him from fulfilling the Word of the Lord. While there's a lot of hooey abounding within the Body claiming that anything short of blind obedience is rebellion, there is a form of rebellion that those chosen and called need never tire of checking themselves on.

The Subtle Snare and the Sin of Witchcraft

This form of rebellion incorporates a point of stumbling that spiritually is extremely subtle: It emanates from the trappings of answered prayer and success. It undermines the will of God and is most deadly when manifesting through those anointed and called.

There is truth in the old adage of a little success being a dangerous thing, because of the tendency it has to distort and blind. Indeed, whether it is an outlook or an attitude, the rebellion that is as the sin of witchcraft reflects a seducing orientation that warrants exposure.

Stubborn Rebellion

Falling short in carrying out the word of the Lord because of a rebellion and stubbornness carried a consequence far worse than murder and adultery. Stubborn rebellion is the worst form of rebellion — because it is a self-righteous rebellion.

The stubborn rebellion referred to in 1 Samuel 15 is subtle because it manifests through and is fueled by the position and anointing of one called by God. It is deadly because the authority of the position sets in motion a distortion to God's initiatives, which significantly impacts others. It is the subtle, but blinding type of rebellion that presumes and pushes into another's sphere, makes adjustments and adversely influences the outcome of something the Lord is in the process of doing.

In Matthew 18:7 of the NAS, Jesus explained it this way: "*...it is inevitable that stumbling blocks come; but woe to the one through whom the stumbling block comes.*"

The Authority Disconnect

So Saul's failure in executing the will of God was summed as rebellion. This is because there is a relationship between authority and faith. Jesus commended the Centurion as having a level of faith He had not seen in all of Israel because as a "*man under authority, who had authority,*" he recognized and responded to Jesus' authority with the type of faith that pleases God (Hebrews 11:6).

The authority connection begins with a bedrock trust in the Lord. It is founded on the premise that God is a good God and a rewarder of those who diligently seek Him. It is based on the knowledge that the Lord is in control and is working all things together for our good. However, there is a vulnerability that impacts the authority connection when one falls short in grasping the depth of God's love and goodness by yielding to an inordinate sin-consciousness that always fears exposure and rejection.

The type of faith needed to please God cannot operate in one who fears rejection and struggles with authority — because authority and faith have their foundations in trust. Trust cannot operate without honor. Honor accepts responsibility and honor bestows respect and recognizes authority. It is reciprocal. Honor falls short in one with a poor self-image. It falls short in those with low trust levels. As in the case of Saul, there is always a struggle to prove oneself, if to no one other than himself.

Without trust, the predisposition is to respond protectively, manipulatively or competitively from the unregenerate soulish realm. Whether due to fear or insecurity or a poor self-concept, the authority disconnect will manifest in presumption, foolishness and rebellion. Without authority, faith is destabilized and on a collision course to becoming an illusion.

Success and Foolishness

Despite his position, Saul presumed to assume a mantel not incorporated in his calling and anointing. The scripture tells us that he acted foolishly.

Saul acted foolishly first, because he failed to give priority to inquiring of the Lord. He was controlled and driven by soulish considerations. He is the prototype of the talented leader who lives by his wits and feelings. Rather than operating from faith to faith and yielding to the anointing, Saul was moving from success to success.

Even within his own sphere, Saul made adjustments to his instructions based on some very wrong reasons. He never got past tripping over his insecure ego in his decisions. Saul needed constant intervention from Samuel because he was blinded by considerations that undermined the will of God.

His modus operandi fell short of the spiritual wisdom and discipline outlined in the instructions for kings and leaders in Deuteronomy 17. He was driven by his concern about how the situation would impact what people thought about him. He continually was forcing issues outside his sphere. In essence, there was a slackness in Saul's approach to the things of God. His spiritual development rather than being personal and intimate was far too vicarious. He knew the words, but was clearly off-tune.

The principle in Deuteronomy designed to maintain spiritual soundness in kings and leaders involves an immersion in God's Word: *"The one who sits on the throne as king, must copy these laws on a scroll for himself in the presence of the priests. He must always keep this copy of the law with him and read it daily as long as he lives. That way he will learn to fear the LORD his God by obeying all the terms of this law. This regular reading will prevent him from becoming proud and acting as if he is above his fellow citizens. It will also prevent him from turning away from these commands in the smallest way. This will ensure that he and his descendants will reign for many generations in Israel."* Deut 17:18-20 Saul's behavior and decision-making as king gave little indication to his making this his practice.

The result was a modus operandi of foolishness that even Saul himself eventually began to recognize, during his latter days as he was chasing David. While he was called and anointed, there is little evidence to support Saul becoming a genuine man of the Spirit. He never quite saw the big picture of what God wanted to do through him.

The Contrast

The book of James speaks of the greater requirements of those called to be leaders. The principles of the Kingdom of God involve the operation of truths that appear as paradoxes to the world's way of doing things. We reign by serving (Mark 10:42-44). We are made great by being the least (Luke 9:48). We are exalted through humility (Matt. 23:12). We become wise through simplicity (1 Cor. 3:18). We become strong through weakness (2 Cor. 12:10). We live by dying (John 12:24-25). We find our life by losing it (Matt. 10:39)

David understood these Kingdom paradoxes. He was a Kingdom leader, whereas Saul didn't appear to have a clue. This is the reason that when confronted with their sin, David was restored and Saul was removed. Despite both being called and anointed, the contrast reflected the difference between a spiritual man and a soulish man.

Saul placed the approval of man before the priority he gave to being approved by God. David was always first and foremost a God-pleaser. Saul's identity was tied to his position, whereas for David it was tied to God. Saul operated primarily by his wits, whereas David by the anointing and in his readiness to inquire of the Lord. Saul was focused on building his own empire, while David had a genuine Kingdom-building perspective. Saul's outlook was a short-term one, whereas David's was eternal. Saul was a self-promoting competitor, who operated in self-serving envy, whereas David operated in humility and flexibility, as a servant-leader. Saul demanded honor, whereas honor followed David. Saul constantly needed the spiritual oversight of the prophet Samuel, whereas David was a spiritual leader in his role as king. Saul's initial response to being confronted with his sin was to quibble and try to cover-up. David's initial response to being confronted with his sin was to repent.

In a word, even when Saul was doing the right thing, his tendency was to do it for the wrong reasons. The story of Saul is a tragedy. It is a tragedy of one called by God whose orientation failed to progress in God-centeredness, a Kingdom-perspective and a Body-orientation, but instead kept slipping deeper and deeper into self-centeredness. It is a tragedy because despite his being anointed and called, Saul's downfall was the result of being seduced by wrong choices — but choices made by Saul and Saul alone.

Two Forms of Seduction

Moral failure is the most obvious form of seduction. Yet among those anointed and called, moral failure is an outward manifestation of a deeper level and more deadly form of seduction. Without in any way downplaying the impact of moral failures, from God's perspective, David's sin was redeemable, whereas Saul's was not.

The sin for each was spiritual in origin. Each had behavioral manifestations. For David, it manifested in adultery and murder. For Saul, his disobedience in failing to wipe out the Amalekites impacted generations to come. But the bottom line for both was spiritual in nature, which David recognized and Saul was blind to. David was the one who without hesitation recognized and acknowledged the spiritual nature of his downfall and radically adjusted his heart. It is why he was restored and Saul removed.

The Tripping Point of Seduction

There is a subtle foundation for the tripping point into spiritual seduction among those called and anointed as spiritual leaders. It involves the snares that seem to manifest with the trappings of answered prayer and the illusions and comforts of success.

In Saul's case, the foundation for his tripping point was nurtured through foolishness and presumption. Rather than operating according to the principles of the Kingdom and facing his weaknesses through God, he sought to mask them. He liked the position and power and never quite grasped the Kingdom perspective needed in the way he operated. Presumption arises from foolishness. Presumption and foolishness represent the seedbed for the rebellion likened unto the sin of witchcraft.

The book of Proverbs is filled with descriptions of how a fool operates. Foolishness is no respecter of persons. It manifests just as readily in the rich, the able and the brilliant. It has its foundations in a soulish blind-spot that eventually evolves into a serious disconnect with God. What's scary among those anointed and called is the deception created by the momentum and perception of past successes. Foolishness and presumption fuel one another. And spiritual presumption has deadly consequences.

Foolishness comes from a drifting heart. Proverbs 4 provides the wisdom needed to avoid the seedbeds that lead to seduction. It tells us to guard our hearts with all diligence, for it is from the heart that the issues of life spring forth. But that same sequence also points to the importance of avoiding deceitful lips and a perverse tongue. Among those anointed and called by God, loose, misguided tongues are a major means the enemy employs to harness the anointing. Loose tongues are a trap that if allowed to go unchecked will lead into a pathway of seduction not unlike that experienced by Saul.

When presumption combines with self-righteous foolishness and issues are forced, premature and damaging judgment can result. *"The Lord does not delay and is not tardy or slow about what He promises, according to some people's conception of slowness, but He is long-suffering (extraordinarily patient) toward you, not desiring that any should perish, but that all should turn to repentance."* (2 Peter 3:9) This stumbling block was evidenced in both Saul and in Judas. It is one that is low on mercy and big on judgment—and blind to what God is doing and the timing factors involved.

A judgmental disposition provokes a caldron of turmoil, confusion and disorder. James 3:16 in the Amplified version describes it: *"For wherever there is jealousy (envy) and contention (rivalry and selfish ambition), there will also be confusion (unrest, disharmony, rebellion) and all sorts of evil and vile practices."* Isaiah 58 reveals the blockage of *"pointing the finger in scorn"* to the blessings of God.

Presumption will modify and compromise the will of God. It approaches things from a human point of view, rather than God's perspective. Presumption fails to inquire of the Lord and attempts to grasp and act on spiritual situations from the limitations of the human intellect. In a word, presumption falls short.

Treading into another's sphere can be through presumption and ignorance. Too often it reflects a blindness incapable of seeing what the Lord is doing through others. The result fails to give honor to where honor is due and creates turfdoms and competition that dishonors the Lord and undermines the unity needed to strengthen the Body and build God's Kingdom.

The anointing is an awesome thing. Yet, as in the case of Saul, there are far too many who presume upon the anointing without the ONGOING INTIMACY required with the Anointer. You don't presume upon the anointing. You don't presume upon the position tied to the anointing. Seeking first His Kingdom and righteousness is an ongoing requisite and discipline for those called and anointed. You don't presume outside your own sphere. The boundaries of the anointing and position are God-defined and not always tied to patterns of success. Holiness is not an achievement or a behavioral pattern. It is the manifestation that comes from operating in that place in His presence.

Bypassing the Snare in Success

The snare in success incorporates an illusion of what the success is and its purpose. Among those anointed and called, success can only be tied to God's initiatives. It is not about a person. Success may bring honor, but honor can neither be sought nor allowed to become the focus. The snare in success is the soulish, blinding response that presumes upon the anointing, distorts the will of God and has a consequence of yielding to the sin of witchcraft.

The rebellion that becomes as witchcraft is a major strategy employed by the evil one. It targets those anointed and called by God. Those serving as leaders in Christian circles are its chief aim. It is a major strategy being unleashed from the lairs of darkness because it harnesses the anointing and undermines throne-room initiatives and major moves of God. The enemy has both the Davids and the Sauls operating within the Body today within the cross-hairs of his sights.

The viciousness of the evil one's strategies have increased because we have entered a time of extreme significance regarding what the Lord is birthing across the earth and in Israel. The stakes have never been higher.

It is also a time to recognize that the avenues for seduction have never been greater. Entertainment, education, information, news, governmental policies, business goals are replete with agendas and pathways of destruction. Yet, God's grace, His presence and the foundations of His Word are the great equalizers to compensate and overcome whatever devilish strategies the evil one may try to throw at God's people.

In the face of genuine God-ordained breakthrough and success, we need to be pressing into the Lord more than during the times when the breakthroughs were being sought. We need not only the requisite grounding in the Word, but the ongoing washing of the Word as a means of inoculation against the high levels of seduction in operation in this era. Similarly, we need to guard against presumption, envy and foolishness; and recognize the boundaries of our spheres, as we give the Lord first priority in our callings to build the Kingdom of God.

"The days are near when every vision will be fulfilled. For I the Lord will speak what I will and it will be fulfilled without delay. For the rebellious shall see that I will fulfill whatever I say declares the Lord. When the people say the visions he sees are for many years from now say, this is what the Lord says, 'none of My Words will be delayed any longer, whatever I say will be fulfilled.'" (Ezekiel 12:22)

CHAPTER 9

SPIRITUAL INTOXICATION

The term "man or woman of God" is normally reserved for one who walks in God's presence and is advancing His Kingdom. Yet, amid those who normally carry this label is a dynamic that shouldn't be so. It is a form of spiritual intoxication; a perversion that mistakes and can displace the work of the Spirit with the results of human effort. It is the consequence of a subtle mix of seduction and idolatry.

The wrong response to the accomplishments or successes of those "doing a work for the Lord" can result in spiritual intoxication. Confusing the work of the Spirit with well-intentioned, but distinctly human effort bears the mark of spiritual intoxication. It releases a contagion and spiritual short-sidedness that can cloud spiritual realities tied to strategic junctures and fresh directions ordained by the Spirit.

Jesus spent a considerable portion of His earthly ministry outlining the principles for those who would serve as facilitators to release "the Kingdom of God." These principles are both the pathway and standard for maintaining the flow of the power of God. They are the fundamental principles of biblical dominion, of ruling over the work of God's hands; and are essential for the unique focus and priorities of the times upon us.

Beyond Human Effort: the Kingdom Distinction

Kingdom principles in many instances are paradoxes to the way the world around us, or for that matter far too many Christian organizations seem to operate. The bottom line is that while we must give God our best; the results that will make a difference will come from that sphere that is beyond our human efforts. It is the reason that again and again, we see incredible things happen through people who don't fit the mold; those we far too frequently judge to be God's most unlikely candidates.

The gift of God operating within us is just that: it is a gift. The scripture tells us: first the natural, then the spiritual. So it is with that unique gift that God has granted to each of those who are known by His Name. It is when we combine that natural gifting with the spiritual gifting, that the anointing truly begins to flow. And when the combined natural and spiritual gifting begin operating under the anointing; it is the basis for the call of God, or what some refer to as our destiny, to begin unfolding.

This is the matrix that operated for Joseph the patriarch at each stage in his tenure in Egypt: in Potiphar's house; in prison; and as second in charge of all of Egypt. It was the foundation for the multiplied impact by which God, through Joseph: simultaneously set in motion an initiative that offset the destruction that was coming upon the earth; brought about His redemptive purposes for His people; and became a blessing to the people of Egypt.

The Shift

So, before us is a similar juncture. The shift is to offset destruction; accomplish God's redemptive purposes; and unveil the Lord through His people to those of the world living under oppression, affliction and sorrow.

As we enter into the shift, the key issue is this: operating beyond our human effort. The Church is crying out for God's power. Yet, it will never see any more than the periphery of His power until it is delivered from its dependence and captivation with the sensory level. When the trappings of success have seduced and thrilled the followers of a church of 14,000 so that everyone is shocked when foundations of sin are laid bare, it is time for serious reevaluation. It is indeed a crossroad from which we must reevaluate our model and standard of success.

Spiritual Seduction and Idolatry

This dynamic—that overshadows and undermines the power of God and clouds the genuine work of the Spirit is not a new thing. It bears uniquely on the Word Revelations gives to the Church at Thyatira:

"To the church in Thyatira. I know all the things you do—your love, your faith, your service, and your endurance. I can see your constant improvement. But I have this against you. You are permitting that Jezebel who calls herself a prophet—to lead my servants astray. She is encouraging them in idolatry and seduction. I gave her time to repent, but she would not turn away from her depravity. So, she will suffer greatly with all those seduced by her, unless they turn away from their spiritual decadence. I will strike her children dead. All the churches will know that I am the one who searches the thoughts and intentions of the heart." Rev 2:18-29

Understanding the profile of a Jezebel begins with the story of the Israelite King Ahab and his trophy-wife, Jezebel. Modern-day Jezebels can be male or female. The problematic personalities are not gender-specific. Simultaneously, the other side of the story was Ahab: the one that Jezebel controlled and "control" is a key word to unmasking them. Ahab, bequeathed the mantle and power he had as King, to Jezebel. The issue with the original Jezebel, as with the Jezebel referred to in Revelation, is the same: power. Jezebels undermine and usurp the power of God. The process reflected by their magnetism, seduction and the consequential idolatry is the same. It results in driving the focus away from God and through spiritual guile, into the realm of human effort and displaced worship. In short, the Jezebels divert and dilute the purposes of God.

The cunning dimension to the operation of the Jezebels is the people-following they create by their enticing, persuasive charms. The even more devilish dimension is the witchcraft that is created by the appeal to the "deeper soulish- and spiritual-levels;" with results from human efforts being embraced, as from God. The Jezebels are the ones in ministry circles who bring spiritual distraction and decadence that diverts people from genuine moves of God.

Discerning Those Operating Outside Their Spheres

The Jezebel spirit brings tragic results by penetrating the sphere of one in authority and then misdirecting that sphere of influence.

For those called to the forefront of God's initiatives, especially those that involve Israel and the extension of God's authority into the marketplace, leadership and direction must come from those anointed and called into these specific spheres; which require discerning those with the specific anointing and authority for these spheres. Discerning the anointing, that bears the authority for the calling, will be evidenced by its fruit.

Maintaining Spiritual Sobriety and Focus

To maintain spiritual sobriety and focus, we need to grasp the subtleties of spiritual intoxication. To intoxicate is to stupefy or excite to where reality loses its focus. Spiritual intoxication is the state in which we become blinded to the spiritual realities happening around us. It is the condition that results from the seed being sown in shallow soil or in the thorns, as outlined in the parable of the sower.

The real targets of spiritual intoxication are not the immature or those young in their faith. Those the enemy would like to ensnare with this tactic are the seasoned warriors who have been paving new ground and making a difference. They are those anticipating the change in the order of the battles and focus before us.

Unto him that much is given, much is required. We can't afford to start coasting or lose our perspective on priorities by letting the cart get before the horse. Otherwise, we'll find ourselves stupefied and befuddled; and even worse, off-course. We need to be alerted to the intoxication from success. Success is illusive and not an end in itself or an indication to take our hand from the plow. Elijah was sent to challenge and bring down the power of Ahab and Jezebel; but more importantly, to sober up the spiritually intoxicated.

The Model and Standard for Success

The goal is not our activities, nor is it our "successes." From the beginning, God made man to rule over the work of His hands in a cooperative, interactive process — together with Him. The model is a God-centered, entrepreneurial one. It is one that brings life, not only in its result, but within the process. It is one that multiplies, not because of our technique, but because we operate as givers of Life.

Jesus was entrepreneurial in His approach. He challenged the status quo and took risks. Faith and risk, when based on time with the Lord, go hand in hand. The growth of the early Church was entrepreneurial until it became institutionalized and stagnated. Revival is always entrepreneurial, with the Holy Spirit driving it. Despite their reputation and outward appearance, the Church at Sardis was rebuked because they had inwardly become dead. So it is when we use the wrong models, as our standard for success.

Our activities and accomplishments must be an outgrowth of that time with Him. The issue demands the level of devotion that comes from being a God-pleaser rather than a man-pleaser. Hearing the voice of the Lord cannot be based on hearsay, gossip or the latest Internet posting. It begins and ends with us individually in that time set aside, spent in His presence.

Spiritual intoxication from being a man-pleaser was at the crux of King Saul's demise. King David also stumbled hard, but not as a man-pleaser. The first words to David from Nathan the prophet targeted the central issue: *"Why did you despise Me?"* David knew immediately. The core to his problem was the relational breach with the Lord.

David, as a shepherd boy, genuinely embraced the heart of God. His calling and many years of spiritual travail and birthing was a consequence of his early days spent in God's presence. Then when the success came, he became intoxicated with what had come to pass from the Hand of the Lord; and began riding the wave and ignoring the Lord. His sin with Bathseba was the result. So it is for us that we are at a juncture and cannot afford to become intoxicated with the blessings and successes the Lord brings our way as stepping-stones into higher-levels of His purposes.

Avoiding Spiritual Intoxication

Spiritual seduction and intoxication also results from the limited prism from which we view what the Spirit is doing. The "successes" within the Western world need to be put in the context of what is happening in the two-thirds of the world with little or no middle class; that part of the world the Psalmist described as experiencing oppression, affliction and sorrow. It will reorient our concept of success and unveil a better grasp of our role, responsibility and connection to those being persecuted and oppressed for their faith.

In avoiding spiritual seduction and intoxication, we likewise need to guard against those we see operating with high levels of manipulation and control; as this potentially undermines the power of God by attempting to do something for God by limited human efforts. The power of God will flow not from human effort, but from spending time in His presence, hearing His voice and becoming dispensers of the anointing that results.

"Not everyone who says to Me, 'Lord, Lord,' shall enter the kingdom of heaven, but he who does the will of My Father. Many will say to Me, 'Lord, have we not prophesied in Your name, cast out demons and done many wonders in Your name?' I will declare to them, 'I never knew you; depart from Me, you who practice lawlessness!" Matt 7:21, 22

Finally, as we double-check our standards of success and priorities, we need to cast down our crowns and present ourselves as living sacrifices. These are times of change. The Lord is removing dead wood from our ranks, reviving us and anointing us for the change.

"To Shebna, I will throw you away violently and there you will die. 'Then it shall be in that day, that I will call My servant Eliakim. I will clothe him with your robe and strengthen him with your belt; I will commit your responsibility into his hand. He shall be a father to the inhabitants of Jerusalem and to the house of Judah. The key of the house of David I will lay on his shoulder; so he shall open, and no one shall shut; and he shall shut, and no one shall open. I will fasten him as a peg in a secure place, and he will become a glorious throne to his father's house. 'They will hang on him all the glory of his father's house.'" Isaiah 22:15-23

CHAPTER 10

THE WEALTH TRANSFER DYNAMIC

"Till the Spirit is poured out from on high, and the desert becomes a fertile field, and the fertile field seems like a forest, justice will dwell in the desert and righteousness live in the fertile field. The fruit of righteousness will be peace; the effect of righteousness will be quietness and confidence forever."
Isaiah 32:15-17

An email I recently received began with: *"ONLY God can bring that kind of synergy, with the Body operating in community as it should."* The reference was to a statement I made about the "exponential."

God's multiplication system triggers the exponential. For believers, the exponential is that God-factor which multiplies the results of our efforts when certain criteria are aligned. It is released when our faith combines with His will and timing; in the context of our serving with our combined gifts in community to advance the Kingdom.

We find our purpose and destiny in the grasp and proper application of our natural and spiritual gifts. They in turn are combined with entrepreneurial and community gifts. The entrepreneurial is God's DNA: to create, innovate and build. When a diversity of our individual gifts is operationally applied in community, something then is released even more potent for us as individuals; but more importantly, to us as a people of God.

So it is, that as a "people of God," we bring about His purposes at a level that far exceeds even the best of our individual efforts. Rightly aligned and applied, this joint effort is the catalyst for the exponential.

However, there also is an exponential that *only God* authorizes. Tied to set-times, the alignment between our gifts and community gives us a taste for and acts as the precursor to the God-actuated exponential. While the exponential that *only God* releases will be marked by times set by the Father's authority, the alliances; along with the shifts in the alignment provide the process that guides us into its pathway.

"It is not for you to know the times or seasons which the Father has set by His own authority." Acts 1:7

Understanding the Times

The Isaiah 32 passage opening this chapter provides a unique glimpse into *a God-only event* before us. It points to a monumental global shift to be released in the Father's timing and authority. It will be marked by God's sovereign intervention that begins the process of restoration from the bondage of corruption.

With justice in the desert describing the containment of evil that has abounded in an unregenerate world; when God's rule and righteousness is restored, the desert will be released to become as a fertile field and those arenas where His righteousness already has root will blossom to a level that will make the fertile fields seem as a forest.

However, the bondage of corruption referred to in Romans 8 continues to run rampant throughout the earth. Yet, as this sequence in Isaiah continues (Isaiah 33:1), it references a time when the destroyers, plunderers, and the betrayers will meet an end for their treachery. So, the expectation remains before us for the revealing of the sons of God, along with the Isaiah 32 outpouring of the Spirit, that creates such a shift that barren lands will be turned into fertile fields and the fertile fields, a forest. It will be an exponential shift.

This Isaiah 32 shift coincides with the time mentioned in Isaiah 60; the prelude to the final clash of all ages, as Israel is restored, the Jewish people return to Israel in mass, with the Lord's intervention and the countdown into the Messianic age.

"Behold, darkness shall cover the earth, and deep darkness the people; but the LORD will arise over you, and His glory will be seen upon you. Gentiles shall come to your light, and kings to the brightness of your rising. Lift up your eyes all around, and see: they all gather together, they come to you; your sons shall come from afar, and your daughters shall be nursed at your side. Then you shall see and become radiant, and your heart shall swell with joy; because the abundance of the sea shall be turned to you, and the wealth of the Gentiles shall come to you." Isaiah 60:2-5

Capturing the attention of believers across the globe, this passage in Isaiah 60 is at the heart of a major prophetic insight referred to as the wealth transfer. The significance of this Isaiah 60 event demands a more *careful grasp of its context,* in discerning the array of prophetic glimmers being advanced.

The Wealth Transfer
The wealth transfer has certainly hit the charts. It has become an accepted part of the lingo of today's pop Christian culture. While the Lord reveals His secrets unto His servants the prophets, the Isaiah 60 wealth transfer represents a throne-room agenda, which must be approached with care and awe.

"For this reason many are weak and sick among you, and many sleep." 1 Cor 11:30

The pattern with emerging throne-room agendas is that before their full appearance, there will be both counterfeits and a mounting of precursors setting the stage for the full manifestation of its sovereign release. We do well then to better define what the wealth transfer incorporates and what it does not.

Wealth Transfer Distortions

The Apostle Paul, explained in Romans 10:2 (Amplified): "*I bear them witness that they have a [certain] zeal and enthusiasm for God, but it is not enlightened and according to [correct and vital] knowledge.*" The zeal and enthusiasm for the wealth transfer indeed needs to be enlightened and tempered, and based on a more accurate understanding. To align ourselves with what the Spirit of the Lord is doing and to avoid counterfeits and false starts, we must recognize the traps that would distort it. The most common misconceptions include the wealth transfer being viewed as a Western phenomenon; of it representing a new slant to individual prosperity; or it having the expectation of a gushing of divine benevolence.

The wealth transfer is not, nor is it driven as a Western phenomenon. The transfer released by the Father's authority will be a global shift that pivots on Israel. As the apple of His eye is mobilized as a people, there will be a transfer of power driven by Isaiah 58 that begins reversing the curse reflected by the bondage of corruption. With over two thirds of the world with little or no middle class and over half the world living on less than $2 a day, the best intentions of the Church and Western humanitarian efforts have fallen short.

While the wealth transfer will certainly involve money and resources, it is not about chasing money or becoming a member of a benevolent breed of nouveau riche. The Western model too often carries a subtle deception that big is better. The wealth transfer will be about serving and bringing transformation through community in a way that shatters the bondage of corruption for the oppressed and persecuted. It is about the type of restoration that mobilizes God's dominion among the "*least of these our brethren.*"

The wealth transfer is not about divine handouts. It will not have its focus as a massive food kitchen, but rather on globally mobilizing the oppressed and afflicted to become the head, rather than the tail; as God's people begin entering the arena of truly ruling over the work of His hands. Tz'dakah is the charitable righteousness that defines God's people. It functions in the context of community by providing the help to enable one to stand on his/her own feet. According to Jewish tradition, the highest form of tz'dakah is helping one start his/her own business.

Wealth Transfer Dynamics

The key dynamics of the wealth transfer include a generational mantle, a community operation and a Kingdom alignment. The mantle for throne room agendas belongs at the generation level. Incorporating a supernatural unity of purpose, amazing things will unfold when entrance to set-times is made by a generation. These amazing things will flow at the community level. The standard set will break the mold and operate against the odds; as God is glorified not only among His people, but among outsiders witnessing the realities of God operating in their midst. The alignment that results will set things in order that have been in chaos and under the bondage of corruption. It will mark the shift in which the Lord's dominion begins to be restored across the earth as His people exercise His authority in both seats of power and in community, to reverse the curse.

Elements of the Wealth Transfer

The key elements of the transfer that will be in evidence will be tz'dakah, a combined top-down and a bottom-up orientation, along with dominion. While tz'dakah means charity, it also means "righteousness," as reflected in the proverb so often quoted in Christian circles: *"Righteousness exalts a nation."* Tz'dakah is the interaction of and entwining of charity and righteousness. 1 Corinthians 13 at its highest level is the righteous charity or charitable righteousness that results when God's people are yielded to Him. It is the dynamic that will be evident through community when God is at its center.

The combined top-down, bottom-up orientation breaks the "big is better" top-down orientation deception that has infiltrated and distorted the foundations of the Western model. Without the appropriate operation of the bottom-up, whether in community, economics, societal transformation or the wealth transfer; there exists an imbalance that undermines the exponential.

"When the first came, they supposed that they would receive more. When they had received the same, they complained saying, 'These last men have worked only one hour, and we have borne the burden and the heat of the day.' But he answered, 'Friend, did you not agree on this amount? Take what is yours and go your way. I

wish to give this last man the same as you. Is it not lawful for me to do what I wish with what I own? Or is your eye evil because I am good?' So the last will be first, and the first last. For many are called, but few chosen.'" Matthew 20: 10-16

In an article I recently authored, I explained that: "From Genesis and the Torah, the Psalms, Proverbs and the Prophets, to the parables of Jesus and the writings of Paul are a multiplicity of scriptures on the bottom-up component of the practical issues of wealth. The Bible contains a richness of wisdom on entrepreneurial practices; on operating a small business; together with principles on how a business grows and prospers. One segment of the Torah in particular, the book of Deuteronomy, is a treasure of principles on how you run a God-centered entrepreneurial community." (http://www.strategicintercession.org/posts/WealthTransferRevisited.htm)

The move of God in the marketplace will offer hope to those who have no hope. Whether from those called as nation-changing Josephs or from everyday entrepreneurs making an impact on their communities, lives will be impacted by this demonstration of the Spirit of the Lord in operation.

When tz'dakah and the combined top-down, bottom-up orientation are aligned, the exponential wealth transfer will reflect and release the momentum to restoring the Lord's dominion across the earth. As the pivotal factor for the Kingdom to function as it was designed, dominion reflects the unencumbered rule of God's authority.

In the same way that the bottom-up economy is the foundation for the top-down economy, so it will be for the wealth transfer. The array of popular top-down wealth transfer venues will be nothing more than a trickle until the bottom-up transfer is fully in motion globally. The exponential wealth transfer described in Isaiah 60 will be actuated at the time the bottom-up transfer has become a grass-roots movement.

"Every man's work shall be made manifest: for the day shall declare it, because it shall be revealed by fire; and the fire shall try every man's work of what sort it is." 1 Corinthians 3:13

The Process and New Mind-Sets

While the eager fervently seek to enter the place of the wealth transfer, there will be no forcing of issues. The process should be recognized for its own value and then refined as God's perspective on the end result is brought into greater clarity and focus.

Far too frequently, the Western expression of the Body is stymied, due to the trappings of its 21st century mind-set. There is a need to break the mold to enter the fullness awaiting us. We would gain much by pausing from the momentum and focus of old mind-sets and past successes, to gain a greater clarity in understanding the times that we may better know what to do. We must embrace the mind-sets that support the biblical foundations of community and the entrepreneurial.

We likewise need to attain a Hebraic mind-set that is so foundational to the truths of scripture. In short, a Hebraic mind-set has a greater orientation to the spirit compared to the intellect. It is far more process versus program oriented. It places greater value on age and wisdom than on information and oratory. It reflects leadership that is relationally driven. A Hebraic mind-set is community-directed, with a true grasp of covenant, as a people. Within that framework, it embraces a cooperative, participatory planning and execution of activities; with an emphasis on the spiritual gifts, service and a charitable focus.

The process toward the wealth transfer is directly tied to the Body coming into the full knowledge of the Lord and operating in unity. *Only God can bring this kind of synergy, with the Body aligned and operating, as it should.* Yet, only through God will it happen.

"You have not passed this way before. So, consecrate yourselves, for the Lord will do wonders among you." Joshua 3:4-5

While the process will align and actuate the exponential in a way that exceeds our expectations; the exponential of the coming shift will be beyond our ability to measure. While even the process will be laced with awe, the global exponential power shift to be released by the Father's authority will bring forth a shaking of the heavens and the earth and the sea and the dry land. It will shake nations.

"He is about to shake the heavens and the earth and to overthrow the thrones of kingdoms; He is about to destroy the strength of the kingdoms of the nations and overthrow them." (Haggai 2:20)

While we as a people of God have entered an arena of bringing about His purposes at a level far beyond our individual efforts; as we globally mature and come together in unity, we need to recognize and correct the gaps in the alignment that will mark the time and the season for this exponential shift.

The move of God underway that extends into the business and community arenas is bridging that gap, as the Body unites and begins dealing with the real issues involved with "being about His business" and in advancing God's Kingdom. The wealth transfer is about a mobilization and power shift that will lead to the greatest time of transformation ...and conflict that the world has ever seen.

"Yet I will lift up My hand to the nations and set up My standard to the peoples; and they will bring your sons in their bosoms, and your daughters will be carried on their shoulders. Kings will be your guardians, and their princesses your nurses ...and you will know that I am the Lord." Isaiah 49:22

CHAPTER 11

HIGH-CALLING REALITIES

"And he said to the king of Israel, Put your hand upon the bow. And he put his hand upon it, and Elisha put his hands upon the king's hands. Then Elisha said, shoot. And he shot. And he said, The Lord's arrow of victory, the arrow of victory over Syria. For you shall smite the Syrians till you have destroyed them. Then he said, take the arrows. And he said to the king of Israel, strike them on the ground. And he struck three times and stopped. And the man of God was angry with him and said, you should have struck five or six times; then you would have struck down Syria until you had destroyed it. But now you shall strike Syria down only three times."
2 Kings 13:16-19 Amplified

Jesus similarly spoke stern words when he said: *"Not everyone who says to Me, 'Lord, Lord,' shall enter the kingdom of heaven, but he who does the will of My Father. Many will say to Me, 'Lord, have we not prophesied in Your name, cast out demons and done many wonders in Your name?' I will declare to them, 'I never knew you; depart from Me, you who practice lawlessness!"* Matt 7:21

We stumble when we fail to face the realities of our callings. Jesus summed up the failure to grasp and follow through in addressing God's will in our spheres as the practice of lawlessness. The fact is that we each are in need of adjusting our mind-sets, facing the realities outside our comfort zones and addressing the "follow-through" of our callings.

King Saul's downfall took root when he failed to heed the Lord's command in destroying the Amalekites and was sidetracked into keeping the best of their herds when the Lord had instructed otherwise. As God's chosen, the book of Romans describes a blindness among the Jewish people regarding their grasp and response to the full significance of their callings. Similarly, as we read the Spirit's admonition to the seven segments of the Church in Revelations, we find the Church with its own issues in responding to high-calling realities.

Throughout His earthly ministry, Jesus used the phrase *"he who has ears to hear"* to describe our grasp of the spiritual, in order to operate in oneness with Him. With the admonitions given to the churches in Revelation 2 and 3, again and again we read *"He who is able to hear, let him listen to and heed what the Spirit is saying."*

The significance from doing the will of God hinges on listening to and heeding what the Spirit is saying. It pivots on the difference between what we might try to do for God and what we allow the Lord to do through us. This bears on maintaining the mode of having ears that hear what the Spirit is saying. Otherwise, we precariously tread a fine line that Jesus warned about when he said: *"I will declare, 'I never knew you; depart from Me, you who practice lawlessness!"* Matt 7:21

A Hard Example

There's a very revealing story in 1 Kings 13 that speaks to this issue. The Lord spoke to a certain prophet to go to the King and speak a specific word of judgment on the reprobate condition of not only his leadership and the declining spiritual condition of Israel, but to note a future leader who would restore Israel to the Lord. It was a word that had both tactical and strategic implications.

With the word the prophet was instructed to speak was the direction that the prophet do nothing apart from what the Lord instructed him, including not going back by the same way, nor stopping to eat or to drink. Just go and impart the word of the Lord and return. Yet something happened that resulted in the young prophet paying an extremely high cost. A lion killed him before his return home. Here's the sequence from 1 Kings 13: 4-22:

"When King Jeroboam heard the man of God, he stretched out his hand, saying, 'Seize him!' Then his hand withered and the altar was split apart. Then the king cried, 'Please entreat the Lord's favor and pray for me, that my hand may be restored.' So his hand was restored. Then the king said, 'Come home with me and I will give you a reward.' But the man of God said to the king,' the Lord commanded me not eat bread, nor drink water, nor return by the same way.' So he left by another route from the way he came to Bethel. On the way, an old prophet came to him and said, 'Come home with me and eat bread, for I too am a prophet and an angel spoke to me to bring you back to my house.' So, as they sat at the table, the word of the LORD came to the old prophet and he cried out, saying, 'Thus says the LORD: Because you have disobeyed the word of the LORD, ate bread, and drank water, your corpse shall not come to the tomb of your fathers.'"

While some conclude that the older prophet simply tricked the younger prophet by getting him to stop and imbibe on the way back; it seems apparent that the younger prophet first erred by praying for the King to have his hand restored. With that misuse of his authority and anointing, the younger prophet undermined the short-term part of his mission and as a result, reaped the consequence. His mission fell short because he failed to grasp the full significance of what the Lord wanted him to do. Whether it was due to bowing to the authority of the King or just unconsciously wanting the King's approval, he fell short when he reversed the judgment that God had rendered to King Jeroboam when his hand withered.

Holding Fast to God's Instruction

This story forewarns those called with high callings to avoid presumption and to spend the necessary time in His presence to fully — tactically and strategically — comprehend the dimensions of what the Lord may be entrusting us to accomplish. God forbid that we should miss the will of God on diversions or waste our efforts and the anointing on superficialities.

Whether it is the example of King Saul, or the young prophet, or the seven churches in Revelations, among those called and anointed with high callings, there exists an enticement to interpret reality through our natural predispositions and worldviews that result in us *"being like everyone else."* It incorporates the temptation to be seduced by fear, short-sided cultural biases or trapped by a self-absorbed blindness. The dynamics of this spiritual myopia may come from our own successes and the need to be recognized; but in reality are blinders to the will of God, serving as pathways of destruction.

Our assignments, as with the recognition of the phases to our callings, need to be adequately bathed and then birthed in our prayer closets.

Models of Facing Reality

The realities and response to operating in Egypt and Babylon, with Chaldea, the wellspring of sorcery in the wings, are incorporated in the lives of Joseph and Daniel. Joseph and Daniel are both models of people of God who had every temptation to "be like everyone else" thrown at them. Likewise, after their promotions, they easily could have been enticed to resign themselves to the "comforts" and conclude the blessings were designed as a "reward" for them.

Yet, both Joseph and Daniel never diverted from the purposes of God. Why? It was because they had conditioned themselves to listen and heed His voice. They each operated at very high levels of prophetic wisdom in their assignments; a level that was recognized as being from God by the people of Egypt and Babylon; while simultaneously reflecting the personal standard in Proverbs 16 that says that *"he who rules his own spirit is mightier than he who takes a city."*

For those called to make a difference, rather than being like everyone else with a Christian sugarcoating, it will take both the prophetic wisdom that comes from God and the mastery of fully ruling your own spirit. The Psalmist described this dynamic of follow-through as it operated in Joseph: *"Until the time that His word came to pass, the word of the Lord tested him."* Ps 105:19

Agents of Change

God gave both Joseph and Daniel wisdom and promotion to be agents of change in pivotal, perilous times. Neither shirked nor fell short of fully embracing both their identity and task as His ambassadors. Regardless of the consequence, they trusted God and didn't vacillate or water down God's will for them in the midst of a world steeped in sorcery and antagonistic to what they stood for. Again and again, they demonstrated the reality of God operating to all those around them.

There is no question that the dominion required for the change the Lord was establishing through them involved strong confrontations with the forces of darkness. Yet, each prevailed and saw God's authority manifest in the midst of Egypt and Babylon's highest centers of power.

There's been a strong word the Spirit has been imparting to the Body, about a shift. God's purposes always involve the restoration of His rule and authority. The shift underway, from a big-picture perspective, gives focus to a transition from the Gospel of Salvation to the Gospel of the Kingdom. It's a shift from the tactical to the strategic. It involves the integration of spiritual, economic and community dimensions of the truths of His Word as the strategy for restoration needed to reverse the curse and break the mold of the darkness trying to cover the earth.

God's will is progressive and uniquely based on what I like to label as the Issachar context: understanding the times and knowing what to do. Joseph and Daniel understood the times and were exceptionally used as instruments of God's purpose, because they knew what to do. They were agents of change, who operated outside the box of the prevailing standards of the worldviews of which they were a part. They understood their authority as lifters of the gates, those facilitating the Lord's entrance into the dominions entrusted to them.

"Lift up your heads, O gates, and be lifted up, O ancient doors, that the King of glory may come in! Who is the King of glory? The Lord strong and mighty, the Lord mighty in battle. Lift up your heads, O gates, and lift them up, O ancient doors, that the King of glory

may come in! Who is the King of glory? The Lord of hosts, You are the King of glory." Psalm 24:6-10.

The lives of Joseph and Daniel are distinctively apart from those enticed by diversions; those Jesus indicated He would tell to depart from Him, because He never *"knew"* them.

The Pivot Point of High Callings

The distinction is based on the progressive will of God that cannot be discerned apart from the Issachar context and hearing God's voice for the place and time in which we live. Anything short of that, hazards on the mold Jesus targeted so often: man-driven religion.

Man-driven religion and the consequence of those lured by it, is what Jesus portrayed as the practice of lawlessness. Jesus described those who would fall into this trap as those who would come to Him, calling Him Lord, demonstrating outward manifestations of the Spirit; yet would miss the significance and purpose of their calling. It is the pivot point of high callings.

Jesus spoke about the importance of understanding the times and the seasons. The parable of the talents yields the context. Those God entrusts with His riches and authority are expected to bring increase and the establishment of His Kingdom rule, based on the level of the gifts imparted. When dealing with high callings, this dynamic is progressive.

The subtle seduction for those with high callings is discerning between the zeal of human effort of what may be "done" for God; and what God is allowed to do through those strategically called, but yielded vessels. That distinction incorporates an ongoing relational connection. Jesus' words *"I never KNEW you"* is the mark of those whose practice fails to listen and heed what the Spirit is saying. The consequence of entering the "practice" of doing your own thing can be deadly, as evidenced by Saul, the young prophet and Judas. James 3:1 warns that there are those who will be judged with a higher standard. In short, high-callings driven by achieving, or anything other than hearing and heeding what the Spirit is saying, is a seductive trap.

Scripture says of Hezekiah, that he did not respond to the Lord according to the benefit done to him, for his heart became proud because of such a spectacular response to his prayer. Therefore there was wrath upon him, as well as upon his people. Yet, Hezekiah knew what it meant to humble himself and repent for the pride of his heart; and in so doing 2 Chronicles 32: 26 tells us that he averted the judgment he had triggered.

Facing the realities of God's will and a high calling will require: time in His presence to avoid operating outside our spheres; time in His presence to avert the misuse of our anointing, gifts and authority; time in His presence to prevent missing the shifts by mistaking stepping stones and strategies for goals; time in His presence to make sure our efforts reflect a sufficient understanding of the times to enable us to facilitate, rather than impede the will of God.

"Lord, You have given me wisdom and might, and made known to me what I asked of You; for there is a God in heaven who reveals secrets and has made known these things." Daniel 2:23,28

"For I have not spoken of my own accord, but the Father who sent me has commanded me what to say and how to say it." John 12:49-50

"Forgetting what lies behind and reaching forward to what lies ahead, I press on toward the goal for the prize of the upward call of God in Christ Jesus." Phil 3:13-14

CHAPTER 12

THE THRONE OF DESTRUCTION

"Joseph is a fruitful bough by a well; his branches run over the wall. The archers have bitterly grieved him, shot at him and hated him." Genesis 49:22-23

A while back, I experienced a very unsettling encounter. It happened in the middle of one night shortly after I had arisen to pray. I had a very strong sense of a powerful demonic presence passing by. Not just a "big" demon. This was a principality, with much power. While it wasn't a faceoff, I was clearly in the wake of this presence. There was an aura of fear and a deadliness to it. But what has unfolded for me since has been an almost overwhelming, crushing burden; and only by immersing myself in God's presence has release ultimately resulted.

In its aftermath and the burden that followed, this experience revealed insights that bear on the times we are entering. Insights into what that presence was, what its purpose is and what needs to be done in response as the Body turns a corner with regard to the times and seasons we are entering.

In the months that followed, as I prayed about this encounter, I began recognizing upsets taking place on a number of fronts in the corporate and ministry arenas where investment opportunities were involved. Ministry-wise, business opportunities set up to fund ministry objectives went array. Corporately, the cleanup of fraudulent accounting procedures crossed the line and extended into the arena of redefining honest opportunity, after the fact.

The bottom line is that there has been a systematic and concerted attack manifesting against opportunities that represent viable revenue stream potential that bear on funding Kingdom initiatives. These assaults extend to attempts to undermine the very economic foundations of the free world. I've previously noted that the segment of Jeremiah 51 that says, *"I will repay Babylon and Chaldea,"* uncovers the age-old operation of mammon and sorcery. Power and witchcraft, in each generation or so, have had a way of creeping into the seats of power that govern the fabric of society — politics, business, the judiciary, education, the media — and seizing dominion.

Today is no different. But what I've begun realizing since my encounter, is that mammon and sorcery have a behind-the-scenes cohort working in concert with their objectives. That cohort is destruction. And destruction works hand in hand with religious spirits and fear. Spirits that carry a semblance of righteousness for those they seek to seduce.

The Psalmist gives reference to a *"throne of destruction, that devises evil by law."* (Psalm 94:20 NAS) One version translates the portion *"devises evil by law,"* with *"devises mischief by decree."* What I experienced in that encounter is tied to the downturn in traditional ministry fund-raising efforts that began back in early 2001. It is also tied to the enemy's plan to undermine initiatives the Lord is setting in motion for the wealth transfer, along with its facilitators, those called as modern-day Josephs.

The Crucible

When light and darkness collide, the situation will be as a crucible for those bearing a torch.

This type of crucible parallels the time that Jesus faced in Gethsemane. Gethsemane means olive press. But it was the steadfast travail of our Lord in that situation that won the victory for everything else that was to follow. Gethsemane was a time in which the evil one's lust for power, along with sorcery and destruction were in full operation as he sought to turn the tide of God's initiatives manifesting upon the earth.

The struggle is over dominion. It's about the building of God's kingdom. But in this struggle over dominion there are issues provoked by the press of the crucible that need to be guarded against for those entrusted as facilitators of God's purposes.

When the pressure is increased, there is a natural propensity for self-preservation. But self-preservation is not a kingdom principle. Jesus taught that unless a seed fall into the ground and die, it will never bear fruit. Likewise, when the heat is turned up, the fruit that remains comes from the type of faithfulness that doesn't compromise or cut corners. Self-preservation tends to lose focus and vision — and can slip into presumption and compromise.

As the struggle with power, sorcery and destruction is increased, so is the temptation for presumption. The crucible and ensuing clashes can result in spiritual smokescreens that give no indication of the way out. No indication, that is except spending time in His presence. These are instances of uncertainty and fear, which give the appearance of the bottom falling out.

Transitions can create this type of uncertainty and fear. But it was in these times, that the Word of God says of Joseph that although *"the archers bitterly grieved him; shot at him and hated him; his bow remained in strength and the arms of his hands were made strong by the hands of the Almighty who helped him."* (Genesis 49) The operation of our faith MUST be based on what God is saying, and not on the circumstances or the presumption that may be provoked by the circumstances. Fear gives way to presumption, and presumption is a trap. It was not fear or uncertainty or presumption or expediency that promoted Joseph to sit along side of Pharaoh. It was faith and the fact that he steadfastly operated in God's revelatory wisdom for that hour.

In guarding against presumption, we need to have a clear recognition of the sphere of our callings. The scripture says that He gives gifts to men. His anointing and those gifts are unique to each of us. They establish who we are in Him, and what our purpose and destiny is while we are here. But our protection is in not only the recognition of, but in operating within the boundaries of our individual spheres. While the scripture tells us that *"they that know their God will be strong and do exploits,"* it is simply wisdom to avoid presumption and operate with a clear understanding of the parameters of our calling. It's enough to count and embrace the costs of our genuine callings without overextending into presumption. Faith does not force issues or operate outside its sphere.

The heat of the crucible can very often trigger compromise. Compromise, fear and expediency can work hand in hand when a situation emerges with no apparent light at the end of the tunnel. Truth faces adversity with courage. It does not give place to fear. The most oft-used phrase in our Lord's earthly ministry was "fear not." Integrity is an unshakeable commitment to truth, without the need to stretch expediency or find any other means that deviates from a straight line. A heart guided by truth is steadfast, obedient and not threatened by circumstances, because it is rightly aligned to the Spirit of Truth.

The struggle created when there is a clash over dominion very often becomes the seedbed for the Judas spirit to manifest. Judas is the prototype of the "double-minded" man, who tries to work spiritual matters out according to wrong motivations and the limitations of their natural understanding. Judas is the epitome of how religious spirits work in the heart of one attempting to do the work of the Lord according to the constraints of their natural abilities. The Judas spirit betrays and destroys. The Judas spirit is driven by fear, and ultimately will be found to be in alliance with destruction. Those driven by it are accusers, yet always seem to have their own dark cloud of destruction that follows them. Despite a time of being energized by the power of their "Judas" role, the time for those seduced by the Judas spirit will fade, and unless they repent, they will themselves succumb to self-destruction.

The work of God's Kingdom is a work of the Spirit, based on God's word: Spirit and truth, working hand in hand. There will be times that require that we face the crucible. When that happens, it is not a time for introspection or guilt. It is not a time to reinvent yourself. It's not a time to get wordy and start venting. Proverbs tells us that *"a fool vents all his feelings, but a wise man holds them back."* The time of the crucible will be for many, times of being a "burden bearer." A time of crushing pressures, that may not always be understood. Yet when this occurs, it is a time to hold steady. It is a time to watch your mouth and hold your tongue! The crucible may provoke despair, but when that happens, it is a time we need to press in even closer to the Lord. A time of dying to self so that that which was begun in the Spirit will not be worked out in the flesh. It is a time to be steadfast in our faith, knowing that He who began a good work in us WILL complete it and bring it to pass. The reason is: that these are times of travail and birthing.

Travail and Birthing

This is a time of transition. While we may see the rumblings of evil at every juncture, the Lord has been preparing His forerunners for the change in wineskins needed to accomplish His purposes for these emerging, pivotal times. And there is no question that these will be times of birthing, creating, and taking dominion as the Kingdom of God is advanced and brought forth in some fresh new exiting ways.

We are God's vessels for dominion — birthing and releasing His righteousness and purposes in the earth. God's very nature is to create. To birth and to build. To give life. And we have entered a time in which the birthing and building is penetrating deeply into the economic and political spheres around the world. This is a new wineskin, as the Body turns a corner as participators in His divine purposes. Psalm 90 tells us *"Let Your work appear to your servants and establish the work of our hands for us, yes, establish the work of our hands."*

The Body is transitioning into a time in which God is building His kingdom. That will involve reclaiming that which is His by penetrating the infrastructures of the world's systems. And the role of God's people in penetrating seats of power with God's purposes in business, government and communication is going to require a paradigm shift in outlook and approach for many within the Body.

There is an anointing to build, to create. When the gift and calling to build and create is tied to building God's kingdom, there is going to be conflict and struggle over dominion. The enemy brings destruction. God brings life and acts of creation. Jacob's blessing upon Joseph revealed this dynamic. *"Joseph is a fruitful bough by a well, his branches run over the wall."* The Joseph anointing is one that bears fruit. It builds and it creates. But the reality of that blessing goes on to say that that gift was not without struggle and confrontation: *"the archers have bitterly grieved him, shot at him and hated him."* But again, the prophetic nature of this blessing reveals the Lord's hand being with Joseph: *"But his bow remained in strength and his arms were made strong by the hand of the Almighty."* (Genesis 49)

A Time of New Wineskins

We are in a time of the crucible. It is a time of significant change. It is a time in which "Babylon and Chaldea," the alliance between mammon, sorcery and destruction are manifesting against opportunities that bear on the creation of revenue streams for Kingdom initiatives. It is a time in which unholy alliances that infiltrate and undermine are targeting modern-day Josephs and wealth transfer initiatives. Their devilish and destructive machinations seek to cripple financial infrastructures based on wholesome, honest means of commerce. Yet the pioneer missionary William Carey concluded from Isaiah 60 that in the latter days commerce would undergird God's initiatives. And the scripture in Jeremiah 51 adds the words, *"I will repay Babylon and Chaldea, says the Lord."* God will intervene and judge the intentions of the mammon-sorcery alliance.

The transition underway is directing us toward a new wineskin. It is a new wineskin in the assumptions governing the Body's perspective on dominion and on funding the work of the ministry. It is a wineskin that bridges the sacred and the secular. It is a wineskin that will penetrate the fabric of society with God's people, initiatives and agendas. But entering the new wineskin will involve confrontation with the forces of darkness — mammon, sorcery and destruction. And the pathway through the transition toward this new wineskin will incorporate the need for a new level of authority that will work in concert with the new wineskin.

The Body has been through two other major changes in wineskins in the last generation. Each has seen significant resistance from within the Church: those who wanted to preserve the old wineskin. The miracle-working meetings of the late forties was a radical departure from the traditional and staid venue most parishioners got from their church services. Then the Holy Spirit revival of the late 60s ushered in a time in which God was taken out of the box — and given a central place in the lives of those touched by His Spirit. What we are now facing is God's penetration of the fabric of society as we simultaneously face the confrontation of good and evil — the clash of civilizations — which will release God's power, incredible revival, and a level of fruitfulness that just may usher in God's end-time harvest.

But the shaking underway should be a wakeup call to the change before us. It should alert us to the need for greater authority for those paving the way into this new venue for advancing His Kingdom. A venue tied to restoring God's dominion. And just as in the days of Joseph, of developing the economic framework to weather or bypass the downturns and reversals that result from the throne of destruction.

The Need for the Fire of Fresh Vision and New Authority

The new wineskin will bring new vision. The old has served its purpose. The new wineskin and fresh vision will be a requisite for those on the leading edge of what the Lord is releasing across the earth.

The face-off over dominion — with the mammon/power-witchcraft-destruction alliance is requiring a new authority from those called into center stage in this clash for power. That will mean a level of holiness that supercedes the status quo and the maintenance of old wineskins.

It will involve the need to understand the times. A need to know what to do. A need to be operating with the fire of the new vision. For those being called as facilitators in this arena, there is a need to understand the difference between the work of the ministry and the building of His Kingdom — as they serve as bridge-builders and restorers of the breach between the sacred and secular.

The new authority needed can only come by time spent in the presence of the Lord. It can only come by operating uniquely by Kingdom principles — the principles that Jesus diligently imparted through His parables during His earthly ministry. It can only come from operating from the perspective of the practical holiness outlined by Psalm 15. That begins by speaking truth in our own hearts. It involves walking with integrity and working righteousness. Of not slandering with our tongue, nor doing evil to our neighbor, nor taking up a reproach against our friend. A Psalm 15 person is also one in whose eyes a reprobate is despised, but who honors those who fear the Lord. The Psalm 15 person swears to their own hurt and does not change. That means they're dependable. They do not put out their money at interest, nor take a bribe against the innocent. Those who do these things will never be shaken.

Those called, genuinely called as modern-day Josephs are governed by the principles in Psalm 15. They've been prepared. They've been through the fire. They're neither tempted by mammon and power; affected by witchcraft or sorcery; nor threatened by destruction.

Yet as we emerge into the time in which God's people are penetrating the seats of power of this world and facilitating the release of the wealth transfer, we will also be entering a time of awe. A time in which to presume is going to be deadly. A time in which to be riding the wave of the momentum of past successes will be a trap. The Josephs are simply not business people with a testimony. The Josephs are called, prepared and anointed as uniquely chosen instruments of God's purpose for these times. They represent the restoration of the "kingly" anointing that governed both communities and Israel as a whole, when God's people of old were rightly aligned with Him. They are chosen as facilitators for God's initiatives for this hour. To build and create. To be a bridge between the sacred and the secular. To impact communities, economies and nations. To bless Israel and open doors for God's initiatives through the Messianic community. To be an extension of the Lord's compassion to the oppressed and needy and widows and orphans. To serve as catalysts for the Lord for both the believing community and those segments of secular society the Lord wants mobilized for His purposes.

Just as in the miracle-working move of God of the late forties and the Holy Spirit revival of the late sixties, there will be those who resist this present move of God: those who will resist bridging the sacred and the secular. But woe to those who are seduced by their own self-righteousness, fear or need for self-preservation: who serve to undermine what the Lord has underway in this present move of God. And woe to the betrayers: those who stand in the pathway of God's initiatives for this hour.

The Wisdom from the Encounter

As I sought the Lord to understand the encounter it has become clear that the enemy is releasing assignments against today's Josephs. There is an attempt to undermine and discredit this move of the Spirit and the initiatives tied to business and investment opportunities designed to fund the unfolding work of His Kingdom.

While there is a serious need for concerted intercession and travail for these resource-generating initiatives to be properly birthed, burden-bearers should also recognize the strategic nature of what is underway and not lose heart. It is not a time to grow weary in well doing; but rather the time to press in and press through.

It is also prudent for those entrusted with these initiatives to exercise maximum caution as they proceed. Those drawn to this arena need to ensure they are called, because the consequences for presumption can be deadly. And for those who ARE called into these agendas, it is time to insure that every "i" is dotted and every "t" is crossed. It is a time to be very discerning and wise concerning decisions, timing and those we choose to labor among us. It is not a time to get antsy or to presume or to force issues. It is not a time to be influenced by circumstances or feelings. Giving first priority to walking in the consciousness of His presence and flowing in His Spirit is a requisite. The time of release and promotion is indeed at hand, but the need for faithfulness, patience and steadfastness at this juncture is just as critical as when Joseph interpreted the dream for the cup-bearer in prison, but then was forgotten for two years. Yet, the delay over the incident with the cup-bearer proved to be very significant when God gave Pharaoh the two troubling dreams: because it became the launch-pad for God's time for Joseph's promotion.

The story of Joseph had at its foundation the fact that God had a covenant people to redeem. Years prior to Joseph's traumatic departure from the land of his people, the treachery of Jacob's sons against the Hivites in their response to Shechem defiling their sister gave rise to destruction having entrance into the land of God's people.

That treachery was still in clear operation when Joseph's brothers debated over killing him, but ultimately sold him into slavery. The compromise and sin of God's people have grave consequences that ultimately must be atoned for. Yet the Lord always provides what is required. But it takes those rightly aligned with him, who are attuned to hear God's voice despite the circumstances. Joseph realized a pivotal issue that needed to be dealt with when his brothers showed up at his doorstep in Egypt. Not only did he create the crucible that brought his brothers to repentance, but he had been ordained as the decision-maker with the authority and resources needed to bypass the intentions of the "throne of destruction" that had been released because of the sins of his brothers.

The Response to the Throne of Destruction

God always has anticipated the operation of the throne of destruction. In the time of Joseph he provided a means of His people bypassing it because of his servant Joseph. In the time of Elijah, the Lord answered the unholy alliance of Ahab and Jezebel: the operation of the *"throne of destruction devising evil by law"* that had penetrated His kingdom with the thunder of His power. The days we have before us will be no different. They will be days of awe.

The arm of the flesh will crumble and fail. There may be times and seasons in which there is a need to *"walk through the valley of the shadow of death."* But the scripture tells us to fear NO evil. For the Lord IS with us. This is an hour in which the forces for God and the forces for evil are being aligned and positioned. There will be confrontations. There will be disruptions and changes to the status quo. But contrary to the time of desperation the church faced in WWII — essentially unprepared — the Lord has been preparing His Body. And He continues to prepare and align us for the times before us.

Despite the strategies the enemy is unleashing, there will be God-given strategies that bypass the downturns and famines, and there will be other instances in which the Lord will answer with the thunder of His power. Uniquely anointed intercessors have been equipped and networked. The awakening and move of God taking place with business leaders and entrepreneurs with kingly anointings and callings and vision is emerging. It is a move of God tied to the issue of dominion and God's people assuming the biblical mandate to *"rule over the work of His hands"* (Genesis 1, Psalm 8; Revelations 4). Modern-day Josephs and Daniels have responded to God's call and are being mobilized, and as they come forth, they will do as Job projected in the midst of his turmoil and: *"laugh at destruction and famine and not be afraid."*

Joseph's time prior to his promotion was as a burden bearer for the Lord's strategic purposes for that day. He steadfastly and faithfully faced the crucible needed for the birthing of the plan and new wineskin God entrusted to him. When his promotion came he became the chief facilitator of the new wineskin that God designed to avoid the destroyer's plans for His chosen people. Those called to pave the way for this current move of God that bridges the sacred and the secular will be facilitators for not only the new wineskin and new vision; but for the release and breakthrough needed as we transition into a time marked by confrontations, but also the outpouring of His power and the restoration of His Kingdom rule.

"Lord, You bring us out of our distresses. You calm the storm, so that its waves are still. Then we are glad because we are quiet; so You guide us to our desired haven. Satisfy us early with Your mercy, that we may rejoice and be glad all our days! Let Your work appear to Your servants, and Your glory to their children. And let the beauty of the LORD our God be upon us, and establish the work of our hands for us; yes, establish the work of our hands." Psalm 107:29-30; Psalm 90:14-17

CHAPTER 13

THE SWIRL

"Have you entered the treasury of snow or have you seen the storehouse of hail which I have reserved for the time of trouble, for the day of battle and war? For the LORD has opened His armory, and brought out the weapons of His indignation; for this is the work of the Lord God of hosts." Job 38: 22,23; Jer 50:25

On October 24, 1996, our 30 year-old daughter Trisha Stemple was brutally murdered. Trish, a beautiful young mother of two, was the administrator for an overseas disaster response ministry and loved the Lord with all her heart. Then, ten year later, on November 6, 2006, Trish's 21 year-old son Shane, our grandson, was killed getting out of his car on a freeway.

The "why" and "if only" questions that bear on the unexpected tragedy of losing a child and then a grandchild involve answers that will only be adequately grasped when we reach eternity. The interim requires a bedrock faith and trust in the Lord, knowing that we live in a fallen world and that there is a battle that rages around us.

Yet, beyond that place of pain and grief, as a prophetic intercessor, in both instances I asked the Lord for an understanding of the context of what was taking place in the heavenlies. The answers I sought are foundational to the calling of a prophetic intercessor: to understand the times and know what to do.

In both instances as I prayed, I realized that the context involved an incredible level of spiritual activity in the heavenlies. When Trisha was killed, the Lord also clearly showed me a serious flaw operating in the Body that plays into empowering the enemy's schemes. I wrote a post for SIGN within days following Trisha's funeral and then reposted it in 2004. It was entitled "Misguided Tongues." It is still pertinent and can be seen at: http://www.strategicintercession.org/articles/MisguidedTongues.htm

After Shane's death, the Lord spoke a very clear word to me about *"spiritual swirls"* in describing the same heightened spiritual activity that was recognized surrounding his mother's death. Likewise, as the evil one has used the misguided tongues of those called into God's service, so the enemy has taken great advantage of the blindness that the Church has for the significance of the days the Lord has decreed to corporately compensate for the evil that rages in this world. The times demand that we better understand the elements of this spiritual dynamic that we will refer to as "the swirl."

Background

Each year the Jewish high holy days precede the counterfeit celebration of Ramadan. The high holy days outlined in the Bible conclude with Yom Kippur, the day-of-atonement. Corporately across the entire Jewish community, Yom Kippur is a time of soul-searching and repentance.

It is no accident that at the time that the great counterfeit religion corporately conjures up a heightened level of spiritual activity at Ramadan, that the Word of God has outlined a sequence of celebrations and cleansing. The Lord has always provided the means by which His people can avoid the spiritual backlash created by the frenetic machinations of God's enemies. Similarly, it is no coincidence that Halloween falls in this same time frame. Many ancient European traditions hold that Halloween began as one of those liminal times of the year when spirits connect with the physical world and when magic is most potent.

God's means of making His people to be the head and not the tail has included the provision needed to compensate for the Chaldeans and Jihadists, along with all the sorceries that run rampant in a fallen world. So, as the Church increasingly becomes reacquainted with its Jewish roots, the times call for a reevaluation of the casual way we have regarded seasons the Lord has set aside to corporately realign His people spiritually. In like fashion, we need to recognize the potential and purpose of the spiritual swirls that manifest during seasons marked by the crazed passions of the enemies of the Lord.

The Swirls

Spiritual swirls bring chaos. They are illusive and major on white being called black and black white. They bring forth the premises that misalign perceptions so that evil is called good and good evil. Swirls mask and shift realities and create illusions and distractions. They hover around anything good tied to Israel, can be counted on to show up whenever a move of God is manifesting or when the enemy's camp is being broached. Swirls can be very subtle and entice on a level that diverts agendas moving toward God's best into something far less. Yet, God brings order out of chaos, which is the truth by which "swirls" will be defeated.

Dealing with the swirls will mean that the Body will have to take a hard step into maturity. The swirls are not only fed, but greatly empowered by the misguided tongues and myopic goals of far too many who are in leadership among the anointed. They bear significantly on how we define "success." Confronting the swirls will take us beyond ethics. Ethics and righteousness cannot be overlooked, but ethics are not enough. Dealing with the swirls will take us beyond simple faith. Again, faith is essential and will be a significant part of dealing with this dynamic. But simple faith alone will not be enough.

Addressing the swirls will begin by hearing the voice of the Lord at a level that is combined with the power of His truths. The pivot point to compensating for this force being released against us will be when the Church begins corporately following the pathway that results in the release of the manifest power of God.

Discerning the Swirl

Discerning the swirls might be best illustrated by describing a rite known as whirling dervishes conducted by a Muslim sect. A dervish is a dancer who stands between the material and cosmic worlds. The dance is part of a mystical ceremony in which the dervish rotates in a precise rhythm. The dancer represents the earth revolving on its axis while orbiting the sun. The purpose of the ritual whirling is for the dervish to empty himself of all distracting thoughts, leading into a frenzied trance or ecstasy that conjures up a power that is released into the operations of its adherents.

The key word in this activity is conjure. To "conjure" means to summon a devil or spirit by magical or supernatural power. It is a means of spiritual conveyance that sends ripples of its impact into its enthusiasts. It is a religious rite that coincides with the activities used in black magic and sorceries. It can involve invoking a spell or a power to influence. Yet, the swirls representing the most damage to the purposes of God are ones birthed in the heart of hell that worm their way and attach themselves within ministry circles. When embraced, the fruit will be hypocrisy, Judas-type infiltration, misguided decision-making and alliances with evil from within the ranks of leaders anointed for God's service.

Understanding the Times and Knowing What To Do

We are entering a time in which closely adhering to the principles and ordinances of God's Word, as well as conforming to the models outlined in the Bible will not be an option. In some cases, it will be the fine line that determines the difference between life and death. Basic Christianity begins with ethical precepts: doing right and doing good. The first steps in Christian maturity involve learning to operate by exercising our faith. Operating in faith on a basic level requires a grasp of basic principles of God's Word.

However, moving into the maturity required for these times will involve a transition into a place to where faith is much more than the outcome of our human efforts. The maturity needed for the days upon us will incorporate a convergence between an ongoing clarity in hearing the voice of the Lord; and operating in a flow, directed by the Spirit of the Lord. This level of constant clarity of hearing God's voice and flowing in His Spirit will be marked and guided by the principles, ordinances and models outlined in God's Word.

Jesus gave us the principles, the model, the pathway and power for change with His teachings on "the Kingdom," which within the context of the Jewish world from which He came, merged the spiritual, community and practical principles of business and work. *It was the pathway and power that would revolutionize and set in motion the restoration of a fallen world.*

Taking this pathway and exercising this power resulted in a handful of His followers releasing the most dramatic societal change ever seen in one generation. It also set in motion a spiritual backlash and "swirls" that resulted in an erosion of both the Kingdom principles and the biblical Jewish foundations so pertinent to this pathway of power.

Understanding the "swirls" will address the feeble condition of the Body of today as a whole, along with our need to face the realities needed to begin moving back into the place of power, that in the days of the early church took only one generation to open the pathway to turning the world upside down.

The quiet of the neighborhoods of the West is an illusion that masks what is currently taking place in spiritual places. The Church in its present condition is largely anemic to deal with the power coming against us. But it doesn't have to be. The same advancements in communications that have allowed the enemies of the Lord to band together and mobilize is available to the Church—and assuming there is a casting down of our sacred crowns and our illusions of success; this "coming together" of the Body will restore both the pathway and power that set the early church in motion.

Confronting the Swirl

Confronting this force coming against us begins with consecration. It will involve a corporate response to the spiritual big picture. From there will manifest the requirement to recognize God's favor in the face of overwhelming adversity and the significance of the strategy of suffering. Overcoming the unleashing of the enemy's corporate power will entail a grass roots focus and genuine servant leadership that has the authority to discern and uphold the Kingdom standard in the face of compromise. It will then come to recognize and begin repossessing the gates of our full inheritance.

Consecration and the Power and Judgment of God.
Consecration involves a time before the Lord that revisits and upgrades our priorities and pathways. The significance of what lies before us is such that we as a Body must prepare our hearts in a level of corporate consecration unlike any time before in this generation. The Lord is mobilizing a band of believers across this world, who will strategically turn the tide of the swirls and this force coming against us. More of the same harder will not be enough. This consecration will unleash the power and judgment of God akin to what was operating in the early Church.

"You have not passed this way before. So, consecrate yourself, for the Lord will do wonders among you." Joshua 3:4-5

The intensity of the battle will require more than our best human efforts and the methods that may have brought results a mere decade or two ago. Again, it is going to take this mobilized band of believers globally to stand as one against the enemy's assaults. Yet, as in the days of Jehoshaphat, God will again and again intervene with His power and judgment to turn the tide, as we stand as one before Him.

"O Lord God, will You not judge them? For we have no power against this force coming against us; nor do we know what to do, but our eyes are upon You. So all Judah stood before the Lord." 2 Chron 20:12

The Corporate Response to the Spiritual Big Picture. The transition needed is nothing short of the Body once again operating according to the principles of the Kingdom that Jesus entrusted to those who led the early Church. It is the power of God that operates beyond human effort. David had a glimpse of this Kingdom dynamic when he described the interaction between the "angels" who wield the power of God to carry out God's plans; with the cooperation of the hosts—those operating now together with that great cloud of witnesses spoken of in Hebrews who are beyond the constraints of time—who are united in orchestrating this divine realignment underway; for the purpose of setting in motion the "works" that will bear on the restoration of the dominion that belongs to the Lord alone.

"Bless the LORD, you His angels, who excel in strength, who do His word, obeying His voice. Bless the LORD, all you His hosts, you ministers of His, who do His pleasure. Bless the LORD, all His works, in all places of His dominion." Psalm 103: 21,22

We who are called by His Name are ambassadors of Life. It is the Spirit who gives Life; and they that know Him MUST know Him in both Spirit and in Truth. The battle that rages in spiritual places is a battle between the forces of Life and the forces of death. Jesus said we would be known by our fruit. Ushering in God's Kingdom will not be marked by human effort, but rather the power of God. There will be no room for leaders with baggage or like Judas, those who are secretly enticed with evil alliances and power. The way of the Kingdom will be a new pathway for many; but will be marked by the power and judgment of God. The principles of the Kingdom demand more—which is where real faith begins and the Power of God lies.

God's Favor in the Face of Adversity. Despite the bondage and oppression of God's people in Egypt, the preparation for the exodus was characterized by an unusual favor not only among the Egyptian people, but at the level of those who served Pharaoh. So it will be as we transition into drawing the line and taking a stand against the forces coming against us.

"Moreover Moses was very great in the land of Egypt, in the sight of Pharaoh's servants and in the sight of the people, so that the LORD gave His people favor in the sight of the Egyptians." Exodus 11:3

Suffering as a Strategy. Biblical suffering is not the result of the messes we create for ourselves, but rather the swirls and pressures that confront us when we're on the right path in terms of God's purposes. Suffering is a byproduct of the clashes that result when the enemy and his minions attempt to undermine our efforts to build God's Kingdom. Becoming a believer during the days of the early Church involved risk and suffering due to its impact on the depravity and oppression prevailing across governmental, economic and religious spheres.

Responded to correctly, the way of suffering actuates the power of God that facilitates the role of world-changers. It is the narrow corridor bordered by Life and death, the delicate passage of which can tip the balance toward Life. There is a significant difference in defensively trying to beat off the enemy and that of "taking up the sword of the Lord" and moving onto the offensive. Scripture tells us that God worked unusual miracles at the hands of Paul. That is because he understood this level of spiritual maturity and the power that is released when we face and embrace the dynamic of suffering as a potent strategy.

The Grass Roots Focus and Servant Leadership. Jesus came and reached out to everyday people. He modeled a very unusual form of leadership by the world's standards—servant leadership. The God-centered entrepreneurial community prototyped by Abraham and outlined in the Torah stood against the oppression and self-serving orientation and corruption that were the typical form of leadership in the world that existed in those days and the world we live in now. God-anointed leadership will always have a grass roots focus, servanthood as its orientation; and be fearless in making a difference in confronting the oppression and evil running rampant in this world.

"Gentile rulers lord over them and their great ones wield their authority. Not so with you. Let him who is the greatest become the least, and the leader as the servant. For I am among you to serve." Luke 22:25-27

Upholding the Kingdom Standard in the Face of Compromise. The power of the swirls is heightened by corner-cutting and falling short of the standards of God's Kingdom that were outlined by Jesus. Blind spots, serious soul issues and compromise have no place among those at the forefront of the battles before us. Psalm 15 refers to *"speaking truth in our own hearts."* The authority and power of God is NOT for those who operate with "issues" or misguided motives. Such are matters to be taken care of in individual prayer closets. As the Body begins confronting the swirls, the Lord will be raising up a generation of leaders who will not fall short of the Kingdom standard. Simultaneously, the Spirit of the Lord will be addressing those leaders who are dead wood, compromising or simply operating according to falsehoods.

Repossessing the Gates and the First Born. Colossians 1:18 refers to Jesus as the *"firstborn from the dead."* Death is the enemy of Life. The early Church entered the gateway through which life was restored to the dead. Today's persecuted church has similar reports. Confronting the swirls will involve recognizing and repossessing the gates of our inheritance. The restoration of His Kingdom begins in this world. Scripture clearly outlines the premise of dominion—which bears on exercising the authority to make a difference as a light in the darkness within the fabric of society. We have entered a time in which nothing less than the standard of *"life from the dead"* should be acceptable. We stand at those gates.

"This is the generation of those who seek You, who seek Your face - even Jacob. Lift up your heads, O gates, and be lifted up, O ancient doors, that the King of glory may come in! Who is the King of glory? The Lord strong and mighty, the Lord mighty in battle. Lift up your heads, O gates, and lift them up, O ancient doors, that the King of glory may come in! Who is the King of glory? The Lord of hosts, You are the King of glory." Psalm 24:6-10

The swirls will only increase until the Western church begins recognizing the gravity of the battle. Coexistence with the evil running rampant outside the peace of our neighborhoods should be repugnant to our sensibilities.

Two thirds of the world lives under the dominion of some form of oppression or corruption. The swirls are the precursors taking their positions against our unstable foundations. The archenemy of the Lord is raising his head in an attempt to close the gap represented by that part of the world where God's Light still remains as a beacon in this creeping darkness. In days past, many of us have heard reference given to "cheap grace." Similarly today, we desperately need the power of God, but because of our "conditions" for embracing the power, it wanes when the sacrifice appears too high.

God's Love is unconditional. Our response can be nothing less. We have the answers. The issue involves the cost and the pathway.

"Lord, You turn my mourning into joy. You comfort me, and make me rejoice from my sorrow." (Jer 31:13) "By Your word O Lord, I have stayed far from the paths of the destroyer." (Ps 17:4) "Lord, You equip me with every good thing to do your will, working in me that which is pleasing in Your sight." (Heb 13:2) "You strengthen me with all power, according to Your glorious might." (Col 1:29)

CHAPTER 14

WHEN INIQUITY STOPS ITS MOUTH

"When they are diminished and brought low through oppression, affliction and sorrow, He pours contempt on princes, and causes them to wander in the wilderness where there is no way; Yet He sets the poor on high, far from affliction, and makes their families like a flock. The righteous see it and rejoice and all iniquity stops its mouth." Psalm 107

Jesus spoke of *"the beginning of sorrows:"* a time marked by wars and rumors of wars and of earthquakes, plagues and famines; a time of great persecution against God's people with great signs coming from the heavens. (Matthew 24:7; Mark 13:8; Luke 21:11)

A mark of our times has been meteorological manifestations that even the secular news media has given repeated reference to as "wicked weather." Despite encouraging steps to fortify and expand freedom; the fact is that global terrorism, AIDS, economic wastelands, and tsunamis and wicked weather are just the tip of the iceberg. They are the rumblings that warn of the emerging of the beginning of sorrows.

The storm clouds brewing in the mid- to late-thirties, with the rise of the Nazi agenda, is an apt parallel to the times before us. Those were days in which far too many were blinded to the realities emerging. Worldwide governmental and church leaders, along with members of the news media sought peace with a formula of explaining away and ignoring the signs of the times — which eventually bore dire consequences of oppression, affliction and sorrow.

Signs of the Times

Today, we again are being pummeled with signs of the times. These are signs that again carry a context of oppression, affliction and sorrow. This year's *"Index of Economic Freedom,"* an effort compiled by the *Wall Street Journal* and *Heritage Foundation,* ranks 155 nations according their economic opportunity and conditions. Burma (Myanmar) and North Korea are ranked 154 and 155 respectively. Indonesia came in at 121. This low figure is despite areas in Indonesia where private enterprise and economic freedom matches the opportunity of many other global markets of the Pacific Rim.

What this means is that Indonesia's economic ranking includes regions reflecting some of the worst economic conditions of any place in the world. Despite scant coverage by the worldwide news media, the fact is that the area hit hardest by the 2004 tsunami in Indonesia has been a beehive of anarchistic hostilities, lawlessness and war-lords, not to speak of the overt oppression of those unfortunate enough to reside there.

We live in a time when kingdoms are rising against kingdoms and nations against nations. Plagues and famines defy the huge expenditures and efforts by well-meaning humanitarians. Wicked weather is all-too-frequently manifesting across the globe. These signs give strong indication of the world entering *"the beginning of sorrows"* spoken of by Jesus.

God's Response to the Cry of the Oppressed

Psalm 107 reveals some very interesting dynamics — and hope that are tied to these troubling manifestations. It is a psalm that speaks of the goodness of the Lord, in the context of the need for redemption and deliverance from the hand of adversity and evil. In verses 33-34 it says: *"He turns rivers into a wilderness and watersprings into dry ground; a fruitful land into barrenness, for the wickedness of those who dwell in it."*

God did not send the 2004 tsunami. However, verse 34 of this psalm does provide a clue into the catalyst of this tragic event: *"for the wickedness of those who dwell in it."*

Verse 35 continues this glimpse into this evil-initiated struggle underway, as God intervenes with His lovingkindness: *"Yet He turns a wilderness into pools of water, and dry land into watersprings. There He makes the hungry dwell, that they may establish a city for a dwelling place and sow fields and plant vineyards, that they may yield a fruitful harvest. He also blesses them, and they multiply greatly; and He does not let their cattle decrease."*

Then in verse 39 the psalmist further explains the context that was outlined in verses 33 and 34: *"When they are diminished and brought low through oppression, affliction and sorrow, He pours contempt on princes, and causes them to wander in the wilderness where there is no way."* One translation renders *"wilderness"* as a *"pathless wastelands."*

Again, we see the response and the unveiling of the goodness of the Lord in verse 40: *"Yet He sets the poor on high, far from affliction, and makes their families like a flock."*

Then, in verse 42, an amazing thing is said: *"The righteous see it and rejoice and all iniquity stops its mouth."*

The Unfolding Drama

Yet before commenting on this significant and very pertinent verse, we need to be aware of some other dynamics unfolding that are tied to this key area so tragically hit by the tsunami. Then we need to look a little closer at the earlier verses in this psalm.

Something very significant was already in motion at the time the tsunami hit. By way of background, AD 2000 was a mission initiative designed to close the gap in reaching every ethnic group in the world by the year 2000. Its premise was based on the fact that far too many missionary efforts were underway in areas with an existing indigenous church, while scores of ethnic groups around the world had none. The organization that has evolved from AD 2000 is called the Transform World initiative. Transform World's aim has been to target a single country each year with worldwide prayer, along with large gatherings that connect and mobilize local believers. The year of the tsunami, their target nation was Indonesia.

Strongholds of Wickedness

There is a level of wickedness that operates on a regional stronghold basis. It is the level of wickedness that holds hostage members of communities and regions. When iniquity runs its course into lawlessness; and lawlessness finds its way into local and regional seats of power; in most instances, that is evidence that a stronghold of wickedness has manifested.

Scriptural economic principles result in a broad middle-class, whereby local communities of believers assist those needing to establish themselves. However, in many nations, there is little by way of a middle-class, with the vast majority of the people oppressed, impoverished and without hope. When this is the case, it is more often than not a stronghold of wickedness that has pushed its oppressiveness to a level that eventually will be confronted by the cries of the people.

As a major breeding-ground for terrorist activities, the Indonesian region hit hardest by the tsunami has long been a prayer target of both local believers and the prayer initiatives of other global groups. As the Transform World initiative for Indonesia unfolded, the dynamics spoken of in Psalm 107 gain clarity and pertinence.

Wickedness devours. It consumes everything it can in its pathway and then looks around for more. Wickedness is a bottomless pit, in terms of its appetite. It feeds on itself. It gains alliances and worms its way into seats of power — then takes over. It also has a voice — which finds affiliation and reverberation in acceptable societal rebellion. There also comes a point when extreme levels of wickedness impact meteorological manifestations.

Yet, there is also a point when wickedness is confronted with a mix of the heart-cry from the oppressed and the mobilization of prayers of believers. The book of Revelations is the story of the final confrontation with wickedness.

Psalm 107 summarizes the conflict and the solution. Scripture tells us that God gives gifts to men. Psalm 107 succinctly outlines those gifts that keep us from being seduced and overcome by evil that devours and evolves into the stronghold called wickedness.

Community

On one level without the Lord, there is anarchy. Yet the Lord has clearly given His own the gift of community, God-centered community.

God-centered community is filled with goodness and satisfaction for those that dwell there.

"They wandered in the wilderness in a desolate way; they found no city to dwell in. Hungry and thirsty, their soul fainted in them. Then they cried to the LORD in their trouble, and He delivered them out of their distresses. He led them forth by the right way, that they might go to a city for a dwelling place. Oh, that men would give thanks to the LORD for His goodness, and for His wonderful works to the children of men! For He satisfies the longing soul, and fills the hungry soul with goodness." Ps 107: 4-9

Righteousness

Another level without the Lord, there is the bondage that is compounded by sin and anarchy. Community without righteousness and God will fall prey to bondage. Righteousness and rebellion cannot coexist. Rebellion despises authority. It lusts for power and creates the confusion and chaos that breeds leaders who pave the way for the shadow of death where the people are bound in infliction and irons. When righteousness is ignored and becomes distorted, deception enters to cloud the perception of reality. No longer will the people rejoice and yield to the benefit of working together for the common good. Without righteousness, the people become slaves to fear and the whims of the power-mongers. The process leads to being overwhelmed and without hope.

The righteousness that comes from God-centered community is marked by freedom.

"They sat in darkness and in the shadow of death, bound in affliction and irons; because they rebelled against the words of God, and despised the counsel of the Most High. Therefore He brought down their heart with labor. They fell down, and there was none to help. Then they cried out to the LORD in their trouble, and He saved them out of their distresses. He brought them out of darkness and the shadow of death, and broke their chains in pieces. Oh,

that men would give thanks to the LORD for His goodness, and for His wonderful works to the children of men! For He has broken the gates of bronze, and cut the bars of iron in two." Psalm 107:10-19

Wisdom and the Supernatural

On still another level without the Lord, iniquity begins to run rampant. It is when godlessness becomes the pathway with fools setting the standard. The Scriptures tells us that God is Spirit and they that serve Him must do so in Spirit and in truth. Wickedness will eventually unveil the counterfeit of compromise, foolishness and the occult. This pathway without the Lord leads to affliction and death.

However, God's pathway involves the balanced mix of Spirit and truth that overcomes the patterns of perversity, lies and sorcery. It is enhanced by the *"sacrifice of thanksgiving"* that reflects the Hebrews 11 faith that acknowledges not only that God is, but that He is a rewarder of those who diligently seek Him.

It is the operation of Spirit and truth that evolves into what the Scriptures refers to as *His works*, which transcend our efforts and are a byproduct of the wisdom and supernatural that only comes from God.

"Fools, because of their transgression, and because of their iniquities, were afflicted. Their soul abhorred all manner of food, and they drew near to the gates of death. Then they cried out to the LORD in their trouble, and He saved them out of their distresses. He sent His word and healed them, and delivered them from their destructions. Oh, that men would give thanks to the LORD for His goodness, and for His wonderful works to the children of men! Let them sacrifice the sacrifices of thanksgiving, and declare His works with rejoicing." Psalm 107:17-22

Dominion

The bottom of the pit without God is when the forces of nature begin rising up and closing in around the efforts of those who lead in the pathway of wickedness. Romans 8:21 speaks of a time when *"creation itself also will be set free from its slavery to corruption..."* and that creation actually *"groans and suffers the pains of child-*

birth," until that time comes. On an individual level, it is the war between the flesh and the Spirit. On a global level, it is the conflict tied to the redemption and restoration of God's creation — through the confrontation and exercise of authority required by those who are known by His Name.

Without God, things are out of control. With Him at the helm, He gives us the authority over the works of His hands.

Entering that level, is indeed a *"desired haven"* in which we can exalt Him in the "community" and marketplace assemblies of the people and praise Him in the "governing" company of the elders.

"Those who go down to the sea in ships, who do business on great waters, they see the works of the LORD, & His wonders in the deep. For He commands and raises the stormy wind, which lifts up the waves of the sea. They mount up to the heavens, they go down again to the depths; their soul melts because of trouble. They reel to & fro & stagger like drunken men, & are at their wits' end. Then they cry out to the LORD in their trouble & He brings them out of their distresses. He calms the storm, so that its waves are still. Then they are glad because they are quiet; so He guides them to their desired haven. Oh, that men would give thanks to the LORD for His goodness and for His wonderful works to the children of men! Let them exalt Him in the assemblies of the peoples, and praise Him in the company of the elders." Ps 107:23-32

There is no question that the area of Indonesia hit hardest by the tsunami has been a spiritual stronghold of wickedness. At the time of the tsunami, it had sunk to the deepest level outlined by the counterfeit parallels to the gifts reflected by a God-centered society. It had evolved into a level of wickedness marked by the mounting efforts of leaders facilitating oppression and affliction upon the people.

The Dynamic

Yet as iniquity snakes its way into and usurps the pathway of a God-centered society — and evolves into wickedness that eventually grows to the place to where the people cry out because of the oppression, affliction and sorrow, this psalm unveils the dynamic that brings hope.

This dynamic involves the collaboration between the poor and needy and lost on the one hand and the righteous on the other, who have cried out to the Lord. Community, righteousness, wisdom and the supernatural, and dominion are not only the gifts bestowed when people come to the end of themselves and recognize and cry out to the Lord. They represent the combined strategy needed to confront and overcome evil on a societal level.

The stronghold of wickedness would never have manifested without the cooperation — be that passive or active — of the people. The people would have never been deceived to allow it without the type of rebellion that turns its head from God. Romans 1:19 indicates that God has made Himself evident to the unbelievers, yet those aligned with iniquity have chosen to suppress these truths. I've heard one definition of the wrath of God simply being the withdrawal of His presence and grace — which allows iniquity to have free-reign.

Gateways for Iniquity

So, this psalm uncovers the gateways undermining the loving-kindness of the Lord. The pathway of iniquity always leads to oppression, affliction and sorrow. Yet the gateway to iniquity is not reserved for only the godless and the foolish. Among the righteous, when principles are compromised in one area in order to follow a "leading" in another, opportunity is given for iniquity to enter.

The balance to temptations for self-righteous compromise is summed up in 1 Corinthians 13 — *"love is patient, love is kind"* — it is not envious or self-seeking. It does not force its own way. Love is foundational for building the Kingdom of God. It was an element severely lacking in the passionate self-righteousness and deception that marked the tragic end of Judas.

Iniquity seeks to infiltrate the inner thoughts and attitudes of the righteous. It is the reason the Psalmist cried out to the Lord asking that the *"the words of my mouth and meditations of my heart might be acceptable in Your sight."* It is the very reason we need to always being prepared to quickly repent and quickly forgive.

Iniquity devours. It is not by accident that Malachi referred to the evil one as the Devourer. Malachi also unveiled a level of iniquity among God's people to where it will take the Lord of Hosts to rebuke the Devourer. While the focus of many within Christendom is to apply these verses in Malachi solely to the economic and financial sphere — the fact is that the Devourer is relentless and unyielding in the spiritual and community spheres of our Kingdom riches as well.

All of which leads us to the pivotal point of this psalm, when *"all iniquity stops its mouth."*

When Iniquity Stops Its Mouth

Terrorism and anarchy work hand in hand. They represent iniquity mobilized and gaining momentum. Terrorism is a stronghold of wickedness that not only supports a global network and subtle underground economy, but it seeks to infiltrate its way into areas that are safe-harbors for righteousness to bloom. It is the ultimate in the pro-active spread of corruption and wickedness. Havens for terrorism will devour the middle class and be a repository for the spread of oppression, affliction and sorrow.

As iniquity devours, it manifests, seduces and masks with counterfeits, the gifts the Lord intends for the people. Instead of a God-centered society, iniquity plants anarchy and rebellion. Where God would bestow righteousness, iniquity undermines with deception, arrogance and lawlessness. Rather than God's wisdom and supernatural, iniquity empowers with foolishness, perversity and witchcraft. Where God enables with revelation and dominion, iniquity releases chaos and destruction.

Indeed, because of the wickedness of those that dwell therein, the Scripture says that rivers are turned into wilderness. Waterspings become dry ground and fruitful land becomes barren. When wickedness is allowed into seats of power and death and destruction begin manifesting, even God's creation begins to draw the line. That is the point when the conflict begins reaching a crescendo. It is also the time when the oppressed and afflicted begin crying out.

It is at that point that this psalm reveals: *"but when the people are diminished and brought low through oppression, affliction and sorrow"* — with anarchy and bondage and with fools resetting the standard — they begin to cry out to the Lord in their trouble. They begin turning to God, where they previously ignored Him or turned away. This is not referring to a trickle, but when the people begin turning to the Lord in mass. So, when the people cry out to the Lord and turn back to God, then the result is *"pouring contempt on princes and causing them to wander in the wilderness where there is no way."*

Then this psalm observes *"...so He sets the poor on high, far from affliction and makes their families like a flock."*

In His mercy, God always hears and delivers. And when His deliverance brings restoration and stability, God bestows His gifts: a strategic mix that combines community, righteousness, wisdom and the supernatural, and dominion. It is then that the Scripture says: *"O that men would give thanks to the Lord for His goodness and for His wonderful works to the children of men."*

THEN the Scripture tells us: *"the righteous see it and rejoice."* When the restoration of the people enters the place of God's blessing and purpose; and converges with the rejoicing of the righteous that results from it all, then **ALL iniquity stops its mouth**.

In a world rumbling with terrorism and oppression and wickedness, there has never been a time when crying out to the Lord for both penetrating the darkness and establishing safe havens has been more important. There has never been a time when reaching out with the comprehensive strategy outlined by this psalm has been more crucial: as God's love is imparted through community, righteousness, wisdom and the supernatural, and dominion. There has never been a time when Paul's admonition of the purposeful outworking of the gifts has been more pertinent: *"...that we should no longer be children, tossed to and fro and carried about with every wind of doctrine, by the trickery of men, in the cunning craftiness of deceitful plotting; but, speaking the truth in love, may grow up in all things into Him who is the head—Christ—from whom the whole body, joined and knit together by what every joint supplies, according to the effective working by which every part does its share, causes growth of the body for the edifying of itself in love."* Ephesians 4

We began by observing that the 2004 tsunami was one of the signs of our times. We began by noting the signs that Jesus described as the beginning of sorrows: wars and rumors of wars, earthquakes, plagues and famines, great persecution against God's people with great signs coming from the heavens. The beginning of sorrows is indeed before us. Yet, we are not without hope or the means to confront the mounting tide of evil and to mobilize the forces of righteousness.

The Strategy Gifts

When we see signs that involve the groaning of creation, we are told our redemption draws nigh. He has given us keys commensurate with the times, with the *strategy gifts* outlined in this unique psalm, if we have the eyes to see how they operate together: **community, righteousness, wisdom and the supernatural, and dominion**. They are the keys that will gag the mouth of iniquity.

They are the keys to the three-fold Kingdom riches of the spiritual, community and the economic, each of which are so desperately needed for this hour.

Despite the storm clouds brewing and the manifestation of darkness across the globe, God's Light will never be extinguished. Malachi 3 speaks of a time of alignment for God's people. From God's stance, that time was a reality-check. It was a reality-check for all the short-sidedness that had been allowed to infiltrate the ranks of even their leaders.

The days upon us are days of awe and days of rapid change. They are days of unusual opportunity and days in which to be alert to what the Spirit of the Lord is saying. If in this time of alignment spoken of by Malachi, the expected result from God's people coming together and turning to Him was the intervention of the Lord of Hosts, Himself, rebuking the Devourer; then, how much more might we expect — as we give focus to aligning our priorities as a globally-connected, mature, mobilized force of those who are called by His Name, in our efforts to confront the darkness and advance the Kingdom of God.

"Whoever is wise will observe these things, and they will understand the lovingkindness of the LORD." Psalm 107:43

SECTION III:

DEFINING THE ISSUES

CHAPTER 15

WITHOUT PRETENSE

"**H**e honored me with his trust."
These words summed up my relationship with my 21 year-old grandson, who was killed in 2006. In his short life, he had been exposed to an inordinate level of hypocrisy and deceit, within a "churchianity" context. His heart-cry was for reality and Truth, which he did find.

Reciprocal trust is foundational to relationships that endure. It's the basis of relational bonding and rapport. Yet, the snare of pretense stymies and undermines relationships that might otherwise be very meaningful.

The American Heritage Dictionary defines pretense as *"the act of pretending, a false appearance or action that deceives; a false show without reality; an outward appearance meant to deceive; artificial behavior adopted to impress others."* In essence, pretense is a veil, a counterfeit to mask reality. Its antonym is "genuineness or sincerity."

The Fear of Man
Proverbs tells us that *"the fear of man"* brings a snare. It's an acceptance thing. More often than not, pretense will be tied to a man-pleasing spirit and fear of rejection. Pretense likewise is the mark of manipulative behavior patterns.

King Saul never quite got it right. His fears and deep-seated insecurities drove him to operate as a man-pleaser. His life was a tragic succession of pretense and being obsessed with outward appearances. Psalm 15 admonishes us to *"speak truth in our own hearts."* If we don't get it right in our own hearts, then we'll never get it right with the Lord or with others.

Jesus illustrated this point with the example of the tax collector and Pharisee. The Pharisee's self-righteous prayer of *"I thank God that I'm not like other men,"* fell short with pretense. Despite his shortcomings, the tax collector's prayer for mercy was deemed worthy to be heard.

Upon first meeting him, Jesus discerned and praised Nathanael as being a man without pretense. Before He ever met Nathanael face-to-face, Jesus pointed out that he already knew him, because the poise of Nathanael's soul was genuine and honest before God.

The one snared by pretense is vulnerable to cycles of betrayal. Their trust is trapped in themselves. It results in a fear that undermines the potential for trust by extending facades, which stir up the potential for the very thing they fear: betrayal.

At Issue

The world is looking for reality. It is looking for the reality of God operating in our midst. To demonstrate the reality of God operating, we've got to be real. As believers, what we extend to others, as the basis of relationship, not to speak of our "witness," cannot have its main focus on us. It involves "listening hearts;" and has to be about God and what He is doing through us.

That's a subtle thing. In an upside-down world, where honor is too often defined by what is achieved, and trust by vanity and soulish superficialities, Jesus hit the issue head-on with the words:

"Take heed what you hear. With the same measure you use, it will be measured to you; and to you who hear, more will be given. For whoever has, to him more will be given; but whoever does not have, even what he has will be taken away." Mark 4: 24-25

These words followed the parable of the sower. They were a key part of Jesus' explanation about how the Kingdom of God operates. If we are going to be genuine ambassadors for His Kingdom, then we can't afford the trap of being self-absorbed or driven by the insecurities that result in us masking the realities of who we are. In the verses just preceding these words of Jesus, He said: *"there is nothing hidden that will not be revealed; and no secret that will not come to light. He who has ears to hear, let him hear."*

Then He made this profound statement in verses 24 and 25 that on first glance, might seem to smack of "double-speak." Yet, what Jesus was imparting here was an incredible gateway into the operational truths of God's Kingdom.

"Take heed what you hear. With the same measure you use, it will be measured to you; and to you who hear, more will be given. For whoever has, to him more will be given; but whoever does not have, even what he has will be taken away." Mark 4: 24-25

The Gateway to Reality

"Take heed what you hear." Proverbs tells us that *"the simple believe every word, but the prudent considers well his steps."* There's a lot of pretense and phoniness abounding in this world. Trust, like truth, is based on reality and must be spiritually discerned, as well as imparted.

Again, it starts with speaking truth and tapping into a genuine grasp of reality in our own hearts. That means, when we enter that place of prayer, we get real. That's foundational to receive what God intends for our lives. The Lord is not going to be shocked or offended; He knows it all anyway.

So, as we take heed what we hear by pushing beyond the facades, then we will grasp a measure of truth, which in turn will be measured back to us.

Going back to the parable of the sower; we reap what we sow in terms of what we grasp and dwell on as "truth;" in other words, what we believe. Additionally, what we reap is impacted by the type of ground into which we sow. What that tells us is those who listen for, discern and grasp reality by "believing truth" are going to have an increase of reality and truth.

Yet, the one operating in pretense, will be losing ground and getting a bad crop; or having it choked out all together. *"For whoever does not have, even what he has will be taken away."*

God's Kingdom rule is based on our role of establishing His authority in our sphere. It's also defined by the extent to which we functionally operate in community. The measure with which we establish His authority will be measured back to us.

Jesus described God's Kingdom as operating like a grain of mustard seed, one of the smallest seeds in existence. Starting small with what you have may seem insignificant, but when it is genuine, it will increase and multiply beyond your expectations.

The Process Counts

What we do along the way is significant. It's with the measure we use, that it will be measured back to us. But it can't be based on false assumptions or pretense.

Knowing the difference between what we might attempt to do for God; and what we allow Him to do through us is the pivot point to entering the place of genuinely operating by the standards of God's Kingdom. It's where miracles and His power reside.

Yet, the systems of the world around us are predicated on illusions that distort reality. During the fifties, a popular book titled *"The Organization Man"* redefined the entrepreneurial foundations found in Scripture. Its message was that organizational conformity was the pathway to corporate success. It implied that institutionalism was a higher standard. Our modern, Western Christian mindsets have been seduced into concluding that the measure defining "Kingdom living" is this standard of Western "success." I'm not against success; but it is not the standard, nor the reality that the world is looking for. The reality resides with us.

The Kingdom of God flourishes in fertile soil based on reality. The seeds are our combined gifts, anointings and callings. To make a difference requires the demonstration of the Kingdom in our everyday lives, being mixed and embedded into fertile soil.

The Point of Stumbling

There's been a shift underway in the heavenlies. This shift has seen a strong emphasis given to the move of God in the marketplace. God is extending His Kingdom authority into the marketplaces and communities of the world.

Yet, far too many with a genuine sense of this move of God in the marketplace have proceeded with an eagerness to "bring to birth" before the set-time. A genuine grasp of what God is doing has been distorted by it being redefined according to warmed-over, outmoded models. The result has been "force-fits" and premature scenarios and flameouts.

Before God restores His Kingdom, the Church needs to face the reality that we fall short when it comes to operating in community. The Church is one of the most fractionalized social movements on the face of the earth. We've become institutionalized and are defined and segmented by intellectual propositions rather than the standard outlined by the Apostle Paul:

"We have this treasure in earthen vessels that the excellence of the power may be of God and not us." 2 Corinthians 4: 7

Far too many outsiders never see the reality of the Lord operating. Instead, the lack of unity and community indict us, with the propositions we hold dear being viewed as hypocritical. We fight among ourselves. We quibble and strain doctrinal gnats, while failing to see the big picture.

The Need and Focus

Before the marketplace movement comes into fullness, the Church must embrace its role as models and builders of community. To do that implies trust. For that trust to manifest, the mold for the old model needs to give way to a Body that is seen by the world as functioning in unity, without pretense.

The issues of reality and trust that we need to grasp as individuals need also to be operating at the community-level. The Church stumbles with the limitations that we tout as progress, based on our 21st century Western priorities, programs and press releases. We fail to recognize that in the majority of the world freedom, as we know it, is at risk. We operate introspectively and with a myopia that is driven by the very factors that blind us and cause us to fall short on this issue of unity and community.

The trappings of success constrain us. We fall short, because of pretense. Our souls are vexed with our cries to see His Kingdom come; yet the bottomless pit of our Western egos can only conceive of that happening through us. The competition and one-upsmanship convict us.

The Lord has been preparing a new thing with this move in the marketplace. With it will be a shift in focus that restores community. That means leaders who break the mold of the Western leadership mind-set defined by upward mobility, social standing and those you know. It calls for leaders who serve, without pretense. The type of leadership that Jesus modeled is sorely lacking. As such, His words apply equally at the community level, as they do to individuals.

"Take heed what you hear. With the same measure you use, it will be measured to you; and to you who hear, more will be given. For whoever has, to him more will be given; but whoever does not have, even what he has will be taken away." Mark 4: 24-25

The book of James deals with issues in a pretty direct way. In the third chapter James describes a wisdom that comes from above that needs to be the tempering dynamic to overcome these points of stumbling. He notes that there comes an arrogance that contends against reality and truth when we entertain and are enticed by bitterness, envy, selfish ambition and what might be summed up as the need to prove ourselves. He goes on to explain that when jealousy and selfish ambition are allowed to reign, that it becomes the seedbed for disorder, confusion and "every evil work."

Again, it's not what we can do for God; it's what we allow Him to do through us.

The plumb line is humility. Trust is the cornerstone. To be seen as real, we've got to be trustworthy. For that to happen, there is a need to remove the pretense and become models of Kingdom trust. There's a world yearning to see the reality of the Lord operating in our midst.

"Everyone will be seasoned with fire, and every sacrifice will be seasoned with salt." Mark 9: 49

CHAPTER 16

THE MOLD

"Don't let the world around you squeeze you into its mold...." Romans 12:2 Phillips

In a time marked by instability and need, the Lord is raising up Kingdom movers and shakers to assume strategic roles of relevance in the world's infrastructures of business and government.

Within that context, a term being heard across a broad spectrum in Christian circles is transformation. It's a good term. Roman 12:2 speaks to the necessity of an individual transformation — of transforming our minds — as a requisite and standard for entering into the fullness of what we refer to as God's will. Transformation also bears on the impact the Body is making on society. While current focus on societal transformation seems to coincide with recent global upheavals and tragedies, it is not without precedent.

The early Church was an incredible agent for transformation. In city after city, most of the leaders Paul selected, as the organizers of this extraordinary movement were new converts from the business community. They faced corruption, witchcraft, religious persecution, oppression and an unstable Roman government. In many ways, the dynamics and setting in the Former Soviet Union represent a close parallel to the risks and hurdles faced by the Church in Paul's day. The challenges both then and now, take courage and boldness, as well as a standard and wisdom by which the Body serves as agents of change.

Combining Excellence and the Power of the Spirit

Jesus taught us that God is glorified when people see a higher standard in our works (Matthew 5:16). Likewise, Paul was constantly admonishing the congregations he founded to operate with excellence. As the transformation process of his day took root, Paul wrote the Body at Corinth to combine excellence with the power of the Spirit in order that this movement not be discredited.

"Working together with Him, we also urge you not to receive the grace of God in vain ... giving no cause for offense in anything, so that the ministry will not be discredited." 2 Corinthians 6:1-3

Paul's exhortation is particularly relevant today, as a mobilization is underway to bring the transforming principles of scripture and the power of the Spirit into the economic, community and national spheres. Yet, the standard in this process of transformation strongly pivots on the J.B. Phillips rendering of Romans 12:2.

"The world around you" — *"squeezing you into ITS mold."*

Pete Holzmann, founder of the International Christian Technologist's Association (www.icta.net) comments on how the *"world around us"* can create blind spots that undermine the standard:

"Throughout history, the church has seen the task as primarily resource-limited, a notion that contradicts the business view of work. Ministries tend to say, 'Here are the (limited) available **resources***, so how much* **time** *is needed to accomplish the desired* **result***?' In contrast, business asks 'we need to accomplish the desired* **result** *by a certain* **time***, so how many* **resources** *(people, funds, etc.) are needed?"*

As a former business owner turned mission strategist who birthed the 10/40 Window concept, Mr. Holzmann is a credible observer.

The Mold

The mold spoken of in Romans 12:2 is just not determined by the ungodly. There is a standard in Christian circles by which we measure what we consider success. All too often it is a standard constrained by the limitations facilitating our own operational "worldview." It has become a mold with limitations that bears closer scrutiny to insure Kingdom efforts are not discredited.

The standard for "success" can be an evolving thing. In the process of change, the measures for success will also change. In Christian circles, if the standard has not kept up with modifications, it digresses into a mold that stifles and sets limits to the results tied to the "good and acceptable and perfect will of God." It bears on the mind-sets that can either release or restrain our walking into higher levels in the purposes and fullness of God. The standard in Christian circles likewise bears on our credibility — and with that, the stewardship of our efforts in building the Kingdom of God.

Understanding the Times

Jesus admonished us to be aware of the times and the seasons. Early in year 2001 a large number of major ministries began seeing significant drops in donations. The speculations as to the reasons for the nosedive in donations ranged from the economy to the aging of the faithful to changes in donor base composition. But despite an array of adjustments by specialists in soliciting donations, the downturn wouldn't go away. Then 9/11 hit. With it came an incredible outpouring of benevolence targeting the victims and the firefighters and those impacted by this terrible tragedy. The result was a further compression of the traditional funding directed toward a wide swath of Christian ministries. Now, years have passed since the early 2001 shaking, without a recovery.

As high profile ministries have faced these challenges, the dichotomy between the forces for God and the forces for evil, in the economic and governmental seats of power, have broadened. Simultaneously, within the Body is emerging a move of God focused on genuinely hearing the voice of God. This move of God parallels a movement of Christian business and governmental leaders intent on using the transforming principles of Scripture and the power of God to make a positive impact on the fabric of society.

The early 2001 shift in the assumptions driving our standard ministry models, combined with the overwhelming need created by the world's burgeoning oppression, corruption and persecution demands a reevaluation of the mold and the standard by which we gauge success. These times call for those anointed as the men of Issachar, *"who understand the times and know what to do."* Likewise, as Paul admonished, we have a responsibility to *"work together, with God, so that the ministry not be discredited."*

This means a review of the realties of our *traditional funding models*, our *standards for success*, as well as the *focus of our efforts*. If the model, appropriate for its time, is aging and becoming a "mold" that constrains and limits, then it is time for change. It just may be that the Spirit of the Lord is positioning us to lift the lid to the mold required to support the work of the ministry when "something more" is in the wings of the wind.

Raising the Standard

The startling observation about Mr. Holzmann's *resource-time-results* conclusion is the amazing results that have transpired among fund-raising supported ministries despite a too frequent lower standard of efficiency in execution. It underscores the potent impact and need for the truths of Scripture and the power of the Spirit. It also begs a stewardship question of what would result if the standard were raised.

We have entered a time in which the world is probing. Some scrutiny is malicious, but some of it is valid. The issue bears not on the growth of the organization, or its PR statistics, or even the good intentions of the faithful — but on the substance behind Mr. Holzmann's *resource-time-results* matrix. It bears on the stewardship of donated funds. In a time when politically-motivated regulators are intimidating, attacking and attempting to condemn entire sectors of business for the sins of a few, we would do well to raise the bar.

This overzealous, scrutinizing trend combined with the shaking in the assumptions driving traditional fund-raising models should be a wake-up call for every organization called to build the Kingdom of God. It was not that many years ago in the eighties when lines were crossed and courts stepped in and Christian leaders were held accountable, as the ministry as a whole was discredited. Despite that, there remains stubborn resistance that confuses the means with the ends — with some who consider the mold that has evolved as an almost untouchable sacred cow.

Proverbs tells us that *the man who excels in his work will stand before kings*. The generation that birthed the Para-church movement is transitioning into the generation that penetrates the seats of power of business and government. As this generation matures and emerges with a role to impact communities and nations, the standard of excellence in the stewardship of building the Kingdom of God must make the transition that will bear the scrutiny of kings.

The standard for Daniel operating in Bablyon was an excellence and wisdom noted by scripture as *"ten times greater"* than his worldly counterparts. Yet, even with that, he wound up in the lions den and his associates in the burning fiery furnace. Their deliverance was because they were without fault. There are indeed ministries, as well as Kingdom businesses with modus operandis that measure up to the standards and excellence suggested by Mr. Holzmann's matrix. There are others that have failed to make the transition, who would never survive the tactics of an Eliot Spitzer or the scrutiny of a 60 Minutes interview with a disgruntled employee, much less the probes of an eager, suspicious investigative reporter.

As the standard for scrutiny has been raised, so have the acceptable standards of excellence and professionalism tied to every sector within Christendom. The stakes and the opportunities before us are such that we cannot be held back by an aging mold. We indeed need God's supernatural intervention more than in any other time in history. The times are such however, that we also need the standard of excellence set during Daniel's tenure in Babylon — of ten times better — to be combined with the supernatural.

The Constraints of the Mold

Every major move of God has been tied to the breaking of outdated molds. Over the years, the Body has cycled itself through searching for that "something more" and the release, relevance and freedom in the Spirit that result from breaking the mold — only to create a new mold that we squeeze ourselves into.

We've indeed entered a time in which "something more" is needed. Yet, the gateway resides with us. Transformation indeed is the key, but it will first require a fresh look at the mold that constrains us. With a fresh look is the need for "something more" in our relevance, methods, standards and execution.

There's an unusual consequence from the shaking going on across the globe. We see undeniable evidence of it from the Middle East to Asia to the Former Soviet Union. The shaking is characterized by changes in economies and governments. Indeed, it represents a shaking described by Haggai many years ago:

"He is about to shake the heavens and the earth and to overthrow the thrones of kingdoms; He is about to destroy the strength of the kingdoms of the nations and overthrow them." Haggai 2:20

While the Body applauds the changes for good, apart from a few, it falls short in recognizing the parallel change needed in the mold that constrains our standards of relevance and excellence and limits our impact. Yet, the shaking is breaking us out of our mold and setting the stage as a new generation of leadership reflects a maturing Body that is returning to the early Church roots as an agent of societal change.

It is a new generation that will restore the focus on Christendom being a movement for change.

Jesus came to bring fulfillment to the purposes of God outlined in the Law and Prophets. God's people of His day were immobilized by a mold. They were fearful, self-absorbed, fragmented, isolated and out of touch. Jesus brought it all out into the open, broke the mold with the command to go INTO ALL the world. Jesus turned the mold into a movement.

Yet, since that time, the natural tendency has been to make new molds with constraints no different from those existing when Jesus first came on the scene. We use the term "planting" churches as a mark of the way the Church-corporate grows. The term "planting" is too static. It engenders a mind-set that falls short of the vibrant spontaneity and mobilization tied to the societal transformation that Jesus set in motion.

Counting the Cost

Jesus taught us to count the costs. Today's move of God in the marketplace will break the mold. A new level of the supernatural will characterize it; that previously has only been evidenced sporadically in this generation. The book of Acts speaks of *"unusual miracles"* being wrought at the hands of Paul. So it will be as this move of God takes the presence and truths of God into the marketplace.

Yet there is a cost. John the revelator spoke of the end-time Church that would confront the forces of evil and the accuser of the brethren with the truth and power of God and *would love not their lives unto death* (Revelations 12:10-11). Jesus summed up the reality of the cost with the truth that, *"greater love has no man, than he lay down his life for his friends."* This was a standard by which the early Church penetrated the world around it on every level. It did so, unafraid. It did so, unrestrained — because of the recognized significance of the movement.

The Mark of the Calling

The eagerness to move to the forefront in this move of God should be tempered with respect for the cost, maturity and realities faced by those anointed and called to lead it. There will be Peters who will be persecuted, imprisoned and then supernaturally released. There will also be Stephens who will pay the ultimate cost as the strongholds on the religious, political and economic infrastructures are confronted, challenged and broken.

No doubt there will be those who seek position and recognition at the forefront without paying the cost, as well as those who seek after the power for the wrong reasons. The story of Annanias and Sapphira in Acts 5 is one of a couple who sought to curry the favor and recognition of the apostles through a large gift, but did so foolishly by crossing the line and tainting it with deceit, manipulation and exaggeration. Likewise, Simon's spiritual immaturity caused him to seek the power of the anointing for the wrong reasons.

> *"He offered them money, saying, 'Give this authority to me as well, so that everyone on whom I lay my hands may receive the Holy Spirit.' Peter replied, 'May your silver perish with you, because you thought you could obtain the gift of God with money! You have no part or portion in this matter, for your heart is not right before God.'"* Acts 8:18-21

The book of Hebrews instructs us on faith. It speaks of those who wallow in the milk of the Word and have been trapped in a mold instead of operating in the maturity that will make a difference. The calling for transformation involves a maturity that approaches the task for the right reasons in the right way. It measures up. It will attract attention, but the Eliot Spitzers and eager beavers in the press will not want to touch it, not only because of the awe, but because of the standard. Societal transformation will involve a massive reclamation. Yet those at the forefront will not be enticed, swayed or tainted as the process brings multiplication to the resource-time-results stewardship standard suggested by Mr. Holzmann. It will reflect a balance between there being no lack and the scriptural admonition that correlates eating with working.

The Dynamics for Transformation

Transformation involves breaking the mold. The days of the early Church were chaotic and oppressive. While religious leaders were playing politics, witchcraft abounded in the marketplace, with the government of the day being evil and corrupt.

Yet, amid the chaos was the demonstration of the power of God. The book of Acts describes it as a time when *"great fear came upon all the Church and upon ALL who heard these things."* So, it will be in this move of God. It's not going to be about programs. It's not going to require hype. It is going to reflect the supernatural power of God in a way that stops people in their tracks — and brings transformation as people recognize and embrace the awesome reality of the God of all ages operating in their midst.

It is time for the fulfillment that has so long been yearned for. Not unlike God's people in Jesus' day, we have become constrained by a mold. The result is far too many in the world around us viewing the Church as self-absorbed, out of touch, fragmented and isolated. Jesus brought it all out into the open and broke the mold with the command to go INTO ALL the world. Yet, we've operated by a standard that is in-bred and designed to bring the world in, rather than us going out. It is a mold that drives our perception of success and the entire way we approach the work of the ministry. It reflects a static mind-set of "planting" rather than it being a vibrant, transforming "movement."

The gateway of societal transformation is before us. Serving as agents of change will take new levels of courage, boldness and maturity, as well as a fresh standard of excellence and wisdom. It will break the mold, as we enter a passage through which the issues of friendship, commitment, sacrifice, integrity and honor take on new dimensions, as the Body faces a task that will bear the scrutiny of kings.

"Satisfy us early with Your mercy, that we may rejoice and be glad all our days! Let Your work appear to Your servants, and Your glory to their children. And let the beauty of the LORD our God be upon us, and establish the work of our hands for us; yes, establish the work of our hands." Psalm 90:14-17

CHAPTER 17

HONOR FALLEN SHORT

"In this manner Absalom acted toward all Israel who came to the king for judgment. So Absalom stole the hearts of the men of Israel." 2 Samuel 15:6

From the time that God has had a people, the evil one has had a parallel quest. That quest pursues the anointing and it targets honor. Undermining both sets the stage for lawlessness. Yet, if he is unable to get them both, the enemy knows he can short-circuit the one by laying claim to the other.

The story of Absalom addresses the issue of honor fallen short. It is the tragic story of one with all the advantages, who misapplied them. Absalom was a man whose potential, in life and history, was short-circuited by disorder, manipulation and slander.

There is an old country expression that illustrates the misuse of what otherwise might be viewed as positive, developing potential. *"Becoming too big for their britches"* describes a person who has stepped outside of what is appropriate for their sphere. The analogy is based on a corollary expression of *"splitting their pants."* The implication is applied most commonly when "showing off "or proceeding in a manner that smacks of disorder, so what results, the *"splitting of one's pants,"* catches the person short by creating exposure and embarrassment that wasn't expected.

Absalom was a man who progressively responded to situations in a manner *"too big for his britches"* by operating outside his sphere and authority. He took bad situations and made them worse. He systematically spread disorder for his own purposes. He manipulated situations to the point of seduction. He ultimately began using his position and the grace of others, together with slander, as a means to achieve his own ends. Absalom not only was a man without honor, his modus operandi served to progressively undermine the honor of his father and king.

"It is inevitable that stumbling blocks come; but woe to that man through whom the stumbling block comes!" Matthew 18:7

The Seedbed that Undermines Honor

Honor pivots on trust. When trust is extended by honor, there are two basic responses based on the heart of the one to whom honor has been extended. Either it will evoke a response to serve or benefit; or as with Absalom, manipulation for personal advantage will result. When disorder, manipulation and slander collide, honor will increasingly be at risk. When disorder, manipulation and slander are allied, then reality is masked and confusion results.

Disorder. Disorder is the seedbed for lawlessness. Those with an apostolic anointing set things in order. That is because it is God's nature to bring order out of chaos, to create and build; while the enemy is the author of confusion and disorder, which ultimately leads to destruction.

Manipulation. Manipulation is the devious management of a situation for one's personal advantage. Manipulation operates outside the proper sphere of authority. It is driven by the fear of man, need for approval, lack of trust and loss of control. Manipulation more often than not employs beguilement and seduction to achieve its ends. Seduction is the enticement away from the proper order of things through the use of deception. It operates in darkness and masks reality and truth.

Slander. Slander involves false, malicious statements that undermine a person's reputation and honor. Gossip, rumor and bad-mouthing ultimately digress into slander. They undermine relationships. They challenge and are at odds with both blessing and truth.

"But even the archangel Michael, when he was disputing with the devil about the body of Moses, did not dare to bring a slanderous accusation against him, but said, 'The Lord rebuke you!' Yet these men speak abusively against whatever they do not understand; and... these are the very things that destroy them. Woe to them! They have taken the way of Cain; they have rushed for profit into Balaam's error; they have been destroyed in Korah's rebellion." Jude 9-11

James 3 lays out the reality of bitterness, envy and selfish ambition being the fertile soil for disorder, confusion and every evil work. Iniquity seduces. The seduction of iniquity is subtle. It entices by degrees. As the grandson of a Syrian king, Absalom's progressive quest for honor, acceptance and power employed disorder, manipulation and slander — all of which combined to create a counterfeit and throne of destruction that put God's purposes at risk.

"Can a throne of destruction, which devises evil by law, be allied with You? They band together against the righteous and condemn the innocent to death. But the LORD has been my defense, and my God the rock of my refuge. He has brought on them their own iniquity and will destroy them in their own wickedness; the LORD our God will cut them off." Psalm 94:20-23

Touching Honor

Despite David's repentance and the judgment of losing the child he conceived in his tryst with Bathsheba, David bore the judgment of Nathan's prophecy of the sword never leaving his house. Yet, Absalom's systematic manner of presuming to touch, malign and then usurp his father's honor brought a backlash of dire consequences. It illustrates the difference between the one who points the finger in scorn and the one who understands the principle of *"standing in the gap."*

Genuine honor, like the anointing, comes from God.

"Blessing and honor and glory and dominion be to Him who sits on the throne, and to the Lamb, forever and ever!" Revelation 5:13

True honor is a God-ordained recognition and respect. Touching honor involves unrighteously maligning or usurping honor. It is expressed by "doing something that dishonors" a person on whom honor has been bestowed. The cost can be high, when the honor has been bestowed by God to serve to the benefit of others.

Dishonor is short sighted. It bruises those in the community that honor was intended to bless. Yet, it relishes in finding the specks in the eyes of others, while being oblivious to the plank in their own eyes. Dishonor is the predisposition to highlight imperfections, while honor is the tendency to perceive and then spotlight God's blueprint in a person or situation.

Touching true honor is outside God's order of things. Apostles establish God's order, rule, authority and dominion for the operation of His Kingdom within their spheres. Establishing God's order, assumes the dynamic of honor and the anointing operating together. As such, undermining honor can undermine the anointing and the establishment of God's purposes. Honor withheld is disruptive to God's order.

"Pay to all what is due them, taxes to whom taxes are due, revenue to whom revenue is due, respect to whom respect is due, honor to whom honor is due." Romans 13:7

Like any other stratagem of the enemy, touching honor can take on a life of its own. Disorder, manipulation and slander are the seedbeds that feed on one another in a way that will lead to usurping or undermining honor. In his letter to the Philippians, the Apostle Paul described his struggle with those who sought to undermine his ministry. He marked those in ministry driven by wrong motives, instead of love. Yet, he admonished the Philippians to do nothing out of envy, selfish ambition or vanity; but to serve in humility by considering others better than themselves.

Gossip, bad-mouthing and participation in the "rumor mill" are base practices and traps that digress into disorder and games of manipulation. Manipulation and deception mask reality and create confusion that sends out ripples that undermine God's intended purposes.

"For I will destroy the wisdom of the wise and set aside the cleverness of the clever." 1 Cor 1:19

There is a false honor. Honor cannot be achieved or bestowed upon one's self. Those who seek honor for their own gain, like Absalom, are skirting the devil's playground. The counterfeit is pride and the power that oppresses and smothers. The world is filled with dictators and oppressors who have laid claim to their positions through deceit, usurping, manipulation and undermining — as they bestow "honor" upon themselves by force, fear and the power of their position.

Contempt and dishonor go hand in hand. Prayers driven by ego, rather than the Spirit are vulnerable to digressing into rants that are aligned with the accuser of the brethren. Mockers and scorners fuel and perpetuate dishonor, while undermining the potential for honor.

"Blessed is the man who walks not in the counsel of the ungodly, nor stands in the path of sinners, nor sits in the seat of the scornful." Psalm 1:1

The Pathway of Honor

True honor treads a pathway of service that doesn't deviate from God's order of things. Honor, integrity and humility go hand in hand. Likewise, honor and favor operate in unison with one another. Genuine honor is far more than one's reputation, although it will certainly reflect reputation. An honorable person is one who can be trusted to do the right thing for others and not compromise or connive.

Honor bestowed is a high level of respect and recognition that usually starts due to merit. It is the interaction between the recognition by others of honor operating in a person; and the mode in which an honorable person extends honor. Honor practiced is the result of consistently operating with the type of moral excellence and service that brings result and benefit to others. The one extending honor to others, while building community, is operating with the heart of God.

Operating in honor is significant because it is a key launch pad for the release of blessing to others. Honor is never self-serving. It incorporates an authority to build for the benefit of the community. It's always other-directed. It's a Kingdom principle.

"Unto him that much is given, much is required; and to whom men have committed much, of him they will ask the more." Luke 5:6,7

Joseph the patriarch was recognized as an honorable man, despite his lowly position as a slave in Potiphar's house and then as a prisoner in the Egyptian jail. Joseph served and did the right thing. The combination of honor and the anointing paved the way for him to sit alongside of Pharaoh.

Honor is not the result of net worth or status, although it may involve these factors. When honor and the anointing merge, the foundation is laid for business as intended by God, with service to the benefit of the community being the linchpin. It is the fruit of the type of leadership that Jesus admonished: that of servant leadership. The mark of genuine leadership combines capability with a fear of the Lord, a heart for truth and a hatred for covetousness (Exodus 18:20).

Despite his many faults and transgressions, David was a man of honor. It is why the Word of God describes David as a man after God's own heart. When he had the opportunity to rid himself of his persecutor, King Saul, David's heart reflected an alignment with the heart of God when he turned away and said, *"I will not touch God's anointed."* 1 Samuel 24:6

The story of Job is the story of a righteous man, a businessman and community builder, who had blessed many people. God took Job from pride to honor. Not only did that involve an incredible revelation of who God is; but it hinged on Job practicing honor at the highest level by praying for the very friends who had dishonored him; and figuratively had kicked him when he was down, when he needed them the most.

Honor will always bear the mark of the wisdom described as from above.

"The wisdom from above is first pure, then peaceable, gentle, reasonable, full of mercy and good fruits, unwavering, without hypocrisy." James 3:17

There is a reason God's Word ordains corporate assemblies beyond that of local gatherings. As we arrive at the time of year marked in His Word as a time of corporate repentance (Yom Kippur), we as a Body have need of examining ourselves. It is for our protection, as well as our release into bearing fruit for the Kingdom. It also involves this issue of honor. We, as a Body, have been dishonored and we have walked in dishonor.

Not only do we need to rend our hearts in repentance for our individual thoughts, attitudes, words and actions that have fallen short and transgressed the pathways of others; but we need to examine those areas that have become snares to us as a Body — that dishonor us as a Body and dishonor the Lord. We corporately need to renounce agreement with and resist disorder, manipulation and slander.

The anointing will never be what it was intended by God, without genuine honor. Likewise, without the anointing, honor will fall short. The maturity of the Body spoken of by Paul in his letter to the Ephesians will not happen apart from honor. When honor and the anointing merge within the context of building community, combined anointings that bring transformation will take root. It is a dominion thing. It reflects the way the Lord intended for the Kingdom of God to work.

"For this is the will of God, that by doing good you may put to silence the ignorance of foolish men." 1 Peter 2:15

CHAPTER 18

HONOR AND INTEGRITY

"For this purpose I labor, striving according to His power, which mightily works within me." Colossians 1:29 NAS

This verse in Colossians describes the Apostle Paul's life purpose strategy: *"Striving according to His power."* That life purpose is summarized in the previous verse: *"That we may present every man complete in Christ."*

Individual spiritual maturity has seen significant progress during this last generation. Incredible levels of substantive teaching have been available due to the information age. Internet communications that link various segments of the Body are now expanding our awareness and strategic outlook.

The process toward Body maturity begins by developing our individual gifts to the level that releases our life purpose. As the individual gifts mature, they are combined to operate together as community gifts. Yet, despite the groundswell of progress individually, maturity at the Body level falls short of the high calling mantle.

A clearer understanding of the myopia short-circuiting Body maturity may require an out-of-the-box viewing of the matter. Identifying constraints and stumbling points that impact those paving the path during transitions are significant to the issue. With the goal of mapping out and building up, it may take only a few glimmers of wisdom to break the barriers of old mind-sets clouding the path for those leading the way into this maturity.

Navigating the Pathway of Change

Despite differences in our approach, there's an interesting overlap in perspective that my wife and I share regarding how individual gifts operate as the foundation for those wielding change. The understanding of the gifts I seek is to find the roots and models of their dynamics outlined by scripture. As a licensed psychotherapist, my wife Carol seeks to understand the roots of an individual's motivational tendencies.

This overlap in understanding how our individual gifts operate begins with a personality test that Carol often administers to her patients. This test helps people define their strengths, so that in a healthy way they can avoid being trapped in their weaknesses.

Perhaps because it describes her own personality, I hear her talk a lot about the personality profile labeled as a "One." Ones strive for perfection. They are high achiever types. A very similar profile is that of the "Performers." Performers are very similar in the results they achieve to the "Ones," except that they are motivated more by ambition, whereas Ones are driven most strongly by their desire to do the right thing. Performers tend more toward conformity, whereas Ones are more out-of-the-box in the way they do things. The difference is between those who produce and those who multiply.

Within the same context, having had friends who have been in professional sports, I have pondered the commonalities and differences found with those I worked with in my service as a career Marine officer. The shared commonalities, of course, are in the discipline and standards of excellence. The key difference, from my experience, might be summed up by my wife's personality profile describing the Ones and the Performers. Performers tend to stall out as they reach plateaus, whereas Ones are continually lifting the lids on the plateaus.

My purpose for describing these profiles is that they have a significant bearing on the issue of societal transformation. This is the goal of Body maturity. Those called as modern-day Josephs and Daniels have callings that not only operate within the context of change, but they serve as catalysts for change. So it is that our response to change demands that we recognize the dynamics not only that bring the best results, but that are operating to ensnare and hold back the change being initiated by the Holy Spirit.

The Mark of a High Calling

Becoming a Christian and understanding what a "calling" is, was not hard for one who had been a career Marine. From the offset, Marine officers are imparted with the responsibility reflected by the words in their commission as an officer that: *"the President of the United States puts special trust and confidence"* in the person being commissioned. Those who embrace the Marine Corps as a career share the common bond of doing so, as a calling. Within that calling and the expectation of excellence that go with being a Marine, are the foundational attributes of honor and integrity.

While the Apostle Paul describes selfish ambition amidst a number of interacting traits on a pathway to evil, ambition itself is not necessarily a negative characteristic. There is an unselfish ambition. Unselfish ambition is often accompanied by zeal. Yet, there is a zeal that scripture refers to *"zeal without knowledge."* The fact is that we have to be in touch with ourselves and with reality to avoid the snares on the path of bearing the mantle of a high calling. To be used by God means we have to be intimately in touch with Him; without the clouding of the perverse forms of ambition. That's where honor and integrity come into play.

On the day that I was sworn into the Marine Corps, the Major who administered the oath asked me to raise my right hand. Then he hesitated before proceeding and looking me square in the eye, said: *"You know that you may be called on to give your life for what you believe in."* I recognized and stated that I did and he went on with swearing me in.

A high calling embraces a cause. Many within the Body operate with a lot of vision, zeal and ambition, but it is the few who have embraced a cause. People will live for a vision, but will die for a cause. So it is, that *"many are called, but few are chosen."*

Honor embraces the cost of the cause. Integrity faces the realities to see it through.

In the early days of our walk with the Lord, we were friends with a couple who were genuine pioneers. They broke the mold and went into some life and death situations and prepared segments of the Body for times of persecution. Before "early-morning" prayer venues became popular in churches, we used to meet early each day with this couple for prayer. They wrote one of the best books on missions that I've yet to read. Few people I had known had either the wisdom or the track record demonstrated by my friend.

A transition then came. This couple stepped back from their role as pioneers, settled in to raise their family and pastor a church. Over time they became popular guests on Christian TV talk shows. Then tragedy hit them with the death of their son. My friend, who had once reflected all the attributes of one following the pathway of the Apostle Paul, spun out. In bitterness, he left the Lord, along with his family. He lost the spiritual balance he had once modeled.

The ambition of his calling, along with the integrity and honor tied to embracing the realities and paying the cost of the cause he had once served, had lost its focus. Operationally, he had shifted from an orientation of being one who lifted the lid on plateaus to one who had peaked out. I still weep in praying for his restoration, yet the truth is sobering: *"many are called, but few are chosen."*

Honor embraces the cost of the cause. Integrity faces the realities to see it through. Holding the course of the high calling pivots on whether the goal is through human effort, or by yielding ourselves to that divine energy that works mightily within us.

The Pathway of the Calling

As he pointed out the importance of the leadership principle of delegation, Moses' father-in-law also succinctly outlined the process that under girds a high calling and life purpose among God's people: *"Teach them the principles and precepts, then show them the pathway in which they must walk and the work that they must do."* (Exodus 18:20)

Understanding the work that we do, must be based not only on the principles and precepts, but in maintaining the right pathway as our life purpose in God unfolds in its completeness. Jesus emphasized this truth bearing on our destiny when He explained that wide is the gate and pathway to destruction, but narrow is the gate and difficult is the way that leads to life. The narrow pathway is the one in which the ambition is on knowing God's heart and flowing in unison with Him. It is the one that brings multiplication rather than just producing.

Maintaining our life purpose is based on the premise that it is not what we can do for God, but rather what we allow Him to do through us. This is the pathway that leads the way into change that makes a difference in terms of God's purposes.

What guides us through this pathway is honor and integrity. Honor is the reflection of the conduct by which we bring credit to the One we serve. *"He who speaks from himself seeks his own glory, but he who seeks the glory of the One who sent is true and no unrighteousness dwells in him."* (John 7: 18-19)

In the Lord, honor will never come from self-promotion, but is only bestowed by God, as we walk out the pathway into our calling: *"No one takes this honor to himself, but he who is called by God."* (Hebrews 5:4)

Integrity is more than simply doing the right thing. Integrity is best explained in Psalm 15 where it refers to being guided by *"speaking truth in your own heart."*

The gateway into the high-calling "work" that we must do pivots on tz'dakah-righteousness. It operates within the context of community. Similarly within the Jewish community are those referred to as "the righteous:" the 'Tzadikim. They are righteous community-builders whose charitable impact makes a difference.

With more than half the scriptures on "righteousness" being within the context of stewardship, this concept of tz'dakah—righteous charity or charitable righteousness, unveils unique insight for the path into our life purpose. It goes far beyond our Western Christian self-improvement programs and what we can do for God. It is released by us flowing in what we allow God to do through us and is the distinctive that determines the difference between the many who are called and the few who are chosen.

The Kingdom Dynamic

What's being described by the words of Paul's life-purpose strategy has its roots in the dynamic that drives the Kingdom. The Kingdom is designed to operate within and bring change to the world's systems. Just as Joseph operated alongside of Pharaoh, the Kingdom doesn't play according to the world's rules. It transforms them. These Kingdom principles often seem contradictory to the natural mind. We wield power by yielding. We gain honor through humility. We lead by serving. We find true life by dying to self. We obtain by giving. They are the keys to the power that transforms.

Body maturity and societal transformation go hand in hand. Societal change will result from Body maturity. This level of change entails paving new ground and a leadership mantle that bears a Kingdom calling. From the beginning, the model for change has encompassed more. A large proportion of the heroes of faith were Kingdom entrepreneurs. As such, business is a means of paving new ground that pivots on change.

The Kingdom model has a combined three-fold foundation of being God-centered, entrepreneurial and community-focused. The Jewish people have been a gift to the world, wielding this model of change. Kingdom entrepreneurship is a strategic tool designed to map a pathway of change. Paving new ground involves breaking old molds that brings about change. In short, entrepreneurship is the art of managing change.

Over the centuries, the Jewish people have served as advisors to kings and been merchants of transformation. Western civilization has its roots in the Jewish Torah. From the Torah have come the foundational principles of the world's most successful governmental, societal, ethical, legal and economic systems.

Like Joseph, who rose to power in Egypt from the most unlikely beginnings of slavery and prison, the clarion call today is for a Body maturity that can take up this mantle of power—with the honor that embraces the cost of the cause and the integrity that faces the realities to see it through.

"We have this treasure in earthen vessels that the excellence of the power may be of God and not of us. We are hard-pressed on every side, yet not crushed; we are perplexed, but not in despair; perse-

cuted, but not forsaken; struck down, but not destroyed—always carrying about in the body the dying of the Lord Jesus, that the life of Jesus also may be manifested in the body." 2 Corinthians 4:7-10

CHAPTER 19

PRIORITY AND OPPORTUNITY

Back in the early eighties, I served on the Political and Public Affairs Committee of one the most powerful trade associations in the energy business. In addressing one of our agendas, the Chairman of the committee and CEO of the Rowan Companies, shared a story. He related that had the Communist governments of the world at that time announced plans to begin hanging all the capitalists in the world; what we could expect — probably the next day — would be a Western rope salesman at their door.

There is nothing wrong with opportunity. Yet, we have entered a season in which those who are called by His Name, both in ministry and in business, need to reevaluate the assumptions. The issue first relates to the Issachar context — of understanding the times and knowing what to do. Understanding the times presumes a perspective based on a realistic worldview. Otherwise, the presumption of knowing what to do will be flawed and fall short.

The issue also has a specific bearing on our priorities and what we consider as opportunity; as we seek to advance God's Kingdom. Unfortunately, the priorities of believers in the West, typically, has little semblance to the priorities of the Body in the two-thirds of the world with little or no middle class. While the Western Body has never been short on charity and philanthropy in its response to the realities faced by those in the rest of the world; yet strategically, the model for transformation, by and large, has been a short-sighted,

Western model, based on a subtle element of Western dependency. It has fallen short in establishing non-Western believers to be the head and not the tail in their own lands. So, the stark realities of oppression and persecution that prevail across the majority of the world remain.

Priority and Opportunity

The Apostle Paul wrote the Galatians about priority and opportunity:

"So then, while we have opportunity, let us do good to all people, but especially to those who are of the household of the faith." Gal 6:10

Paul made it very clear, that within the context of taking advantage of opportunity, our first priority is to build up the household of faith. That principle is modeled throughout both the Old and New Covenants.

During the mid-nineties, I penned my first article about a calling of modern-day Josephs, who, like Joseph the patriarch, would play a significant role in addressing a time of crisis coming upon the earth. However, the model being embraced by far too many for today's Joseph calling, with its anticipated role in administrating resources and power in a time of crisis, is yielding to an outdated, Western-dependent, ministry wineskin. The fact is that outside the Western world, the majority of the people live in crisis and the reality of the opportunities is being blinded by our outmoded mind-sets.

To start recognizing the opportunities in order to make a difference where there is crisis, the current move of God in the marketplace is going to have to begin challenging the precepts of both our worldview and the standards by which we are ascribing our priorities. Modern-day Josephs must be at the epicenter in recognizing these opportunities as the Body awakens to the plight of the brethren living in crisis, persecution and oppression.

I've previously written that the wealth transfer is not about money. While it may involve money, the wealth transfer will be part of the prelude to the clash of all ages. The clash of all ages will pivot on Israel and extend worldwide — and be focused around the restoration of God's redemptive dominion and order.

It is this restoration of the operation of God's authority that will unleash societal transformation. Central to the reorientation will be a shift from the Gospel of Salvation that has prevailed in the Western mind-set in recent generations, to the Gospel of the Kingdom.

The Gospel of the Kingdom

The Gospel of the Kingdom will by no means overlook the focus on salvation. In reality, it will enhance it. However, the issue relates to realigning our approach to what was described in Acts 17 as *"turning the world upside down."* The issue relates to change. Central to the change needed for transformation that builds the Kingdom, will be the new-wine skin orientation of how we respond to prioritizing opportunity.

During the same time frame that my friend from the Rowan Companies was commenting on misguided opportunism, Apple Computer's founder Steve Jobs challenged Pepsi's vice-president John Sculley (the man who orchestrated the Pepsi Challenge) with these words: *"Do you want to spend the rest of your life selling sugared water or do you want to change the world?"* That question strips the superficialities from our notions of success and really hits the priority nail on the head. Every modern-day Joseph should be embracing opportunity within this context and operating as a change-artist, to actively change the world in the sphere of their calling.

Realities, Opportunity and Focus

Margaret Thatcher once commented that Ronald Reagan *"ended the cold war and made the world safer for democracy and capitalism."* While I agree, my prayer is that the path he paved was for something more significant than opportunity for the capitalist rope peddlers. My prayer also, is that those emerging as today's Josephs are genuinely facing the realities operating outside the sphere of the West; and that they have enough of a strategic outlook to see the priority of mobilizing and building up those who are of the household of faith in these lands.

"So then, while we have opportunity, let us do good to all people, but especially to those who are of the household of the faith." Gal 6:10

Unfortunately, many sincere Western Christians, in both ministry and business, in their old wineskin zeal, unwittingly prop up and perpetuate the very systems and organizations that persecute and oppress those of the household of faith in the lands in which they find opportunity. It may not be selling the rope to hang the capitalists, but if it doesn't build up the believing community in lands of oppression and persecution, then it is flawed and falls short.

Jesus spent a lot of time with His disciples imparting the principles of faith. Faith is both a relational and an operational thing. Relationally with God, it first involves moving outside the boundaries of our sensory levels and into the spiritual realm, which is uniquely tied to our operating in oneness with the Lord and His priorities. That in turn is the gateway into the second relational dimension, as we employ our gifts and callings to serve as God's ambassadors in making a difference for those around us. With that foundation, operationally, faith is tied to dominion; to redeeming and restoring God's authority and purposes into the peoples and systems of the earth.

Catalysts for Change

What Jesus prepared His disciples with, were the principles to bring change; the type of change that would restore God's order and dominion. It all begins with faith and extends into those wonderful principles of His Kingdom that so often contradict what we view as the "natural" order of things. The fact is that spirit controls matter and is the foundation for the authority to restore God's Kingdom rule. The words of Jesus, as well as those of Paul call for a breaking of the mold, both from the worldly standard, as well as from the religious standard. We need to recapture the wineskin-for-change that got diverted from the momentum established by the first century Church.

The early Church was referred to as those who were turning the world upside down. Turning the world upside down today is not going to happen by blindly importing and leveraging Western expertise and funds into lands of oppression and persecution; or by schmoozing the local Herod's and Pharisees. It's going to happen strategically, from within; by mobilizing and equipping local believers as agents of change who will take dominion in their own lands.

"So then, while we have opportunity, let us do good to all people, but especially to those who are of the household of the faith." Gal 6:10

Joseph was totally integrated into Egyptian society, to the degree that his brothers didn't recognize him until he chose to reveal himself to them. He was faithful in administrating the authority entrusted to him, at each operational level, during his tenure in Egypt. God is not looking for rope peddlers to serve as benevolent, modern-day Josephs. Like Joseph the patriarch, the calling today is completely outside the box of what may have been previously acceptable operating parameters. This bears significantly on how we approach opportunity for change, based on our priorities.

The Seduction of Power

Today's apostles of change are at the helm in a huge power-shift. It is a power shift that challenges the combined status quo of the spiritual, community and economic dimensions that govern entire societies. Unfortunately, power seduces, blinds and corrupts. If it is not the seduction of responding to opportunity to selling rope to those who intend to hang the capitalists; it is the outmoded wineskin adages that limit the outlook and keep the Josephs operating passively in setting the agendas. In reality we are entering a time in which modern-day Josephs, as catalysts for change, are being called to the forefront of releasing spiritual, community and economic initiatives in arenas of crisis.

This is why the Joseph calling will not operate outside the cloak of humility. It is a calling that excludes the ministry-circle social climbers and those who encourage it. It excludes those who actively or passively abuse their authority; or give place to condescension and the subtleties of spiritual snobbery. Humility was foundational for everything that Joseph was called to do. Humility, among those with this high calling, cannot be achieved outside of recognizing our complete inability to accomplish God's purposes, aside from Him. The difference between operating in a mode of "what we can do for God," and what He is allowed to do through us, is not just subtle, but of such significance that it will impact the results for eternity.

The Gateway to Opportunity: Redirecting Priorities

Joseph stood alone in his calling. His promotion did not come as a result of his efforts or righteousness. It was certainly not the result of Potiphar's prayers. Nor was it the result of the cupbearer remembering to intervene. Joseph yielded to God's calling at every step. His promotion came directly from the Lord at a critical juncture in time when there would be no question of the priorities penetrating the opportunity with pinpoint precision. God was the One who put things in order and established the timing with the dreams He gave Pharaoh.

Joseph's agendas, when sitting along side of Pharaoh, became the gateway through which God re-navigated and set the stage for His purposes for His people Israel for all eternity, while blessing the peoples around them in the process.

The reality is that both the crisis and the foundation for the long-awaited wealth transfer are upon us. The issue is one of dispersing and dispensing. There is a need to disperse the smokescreens that enshroud the priorities tied to entering the gateway to mobilize national believers to become the head and not the tail in lands of affliction and oppression. With that alignment will come the opportunities to begin dispensing the wealth.

"So then, while we have opportunity, let us do good to all people, but especially to those who are of the household of the faith." Gal 6:10

The question to those in ministry is this: When the fire passes from the burning of the chaff (Matt 3:12), what is it that will remain for your efforts? Will you be known as using your gifts and resources to build up the Body to tangibly impact those parts of the world where corruption, distress and affliction prevail?

Then to the modern-day Josephs, the question is: What will your legacy be? When the Lord separates the sheep and the goats, will eternity see you as one who provided the rope for those undermining the causes of God's Kingdom; or will you use your resources to mobilize and equip the brethren in lands of oppression and persecution.

And for each of us, the question is what have we done about the apple of His eye, the Jewish people? May the Lord individually give us the revelation and grace: to ensure our focus and priorities are on the opportunities and goals that serve the purposes of the One who sees in secret; rather than on the recognition and praise that come from the short-sighted worldviews and perspectives that gain the approval of men.

"And He will answer them and say, inasmuch as you did it to the least of these My brethren, you did it to Me." Matthew 25:50

CHAPTER 20

PIERCING THE VEIL

"But the Samaritans did not receive Him, as His face was set toward Jerusalem. So James and John asked, 'Lord, do you not want us to command fire from heaven to consume them?' But Jesus rebuked them and said, 'you do not know of what sort of spirit you are, for the Son of Man did not come to destroy men's lives, but to save them.'" Luke 9: 53-55

The times are turbulent. They demand something more. The mark of a high calling is not just a grasp of the times, but knowing what to do. Knowing what to do will begin by clearly discerning the realities and subtleties that are masked and entwined.

Knowing what to do will involve distinguishing and penetrating a dimension best described as a veil. There is a veil between soul and spirit; one between light and darkness, as well as a veil between the natural and supernatural.

The dictionary describes "veil" as *a covering that conceals or disguises*. A spiritual veil is a dimension or barrier that cannot be penetrated with human effort. This spiritual barrier may be due to a blindness, a hindrance, a threshold to be surmounted, or an alignment or timing factor to bring release or change from the Lord.

Discerning the Veil

When facing a spiritual threshold, discerning the veil is the first step in the process of it being pierced. Veils can be of God's design or implanted by the enemy.

God's Veils. God's veils characteristically allow for spiritual alignment and the prevention of premature actions. They enable the full impact for the God-initiated release. After interpreting the dream for the cupbearer, Joseph confronted a veil that remained in place until the set-time for his promotion.

Since the time of Jesus' earthly ministry, His followers too often have had the tendency toward missing the big picture and getting sidetracked with their short-sighted spiritual conclusions. James and John illustrated this in Luke 9. Jesus distinguished Elijah's action of calling down the fire — from their suggestion of judging the Samaritan's rejection of Jesus. James' and John's premature judgment not only fell short in grasping the purpose for implementing the power of God; but it would have created a diversion from Jesus having set his face toward Jerusalem in the greatest veil piercing of all time.

Enemy Veils. In an increasing number of modern-day cases, veils implanted by the evil one create diversions targeting higher-level Kingdom advances. One of the most diabolical strategies against Kingdom agendas is *embedded evil*. Whether the result of wolves in sheep's clothing or simply sick sheep who have wormed their way into ministry decision-circles, the enemy specializes in infiltrators; "plants" embedded within leadership circles whose purpose it is to divert and undermine the work of the Kingdom.

David Davis in his book *"Road to Carmel,"* tells of a time great advances were being made in his ministry's efforts. Volunteers he describes as modern-day Jezebels and Ahabs began infiltrating the ranks of his ministry. The interlopers were ones who talked the talk, but whose real intention was to get close to those operating in the power and anointing of God.

These hyper-spiritual plants are typically without a viable track record of their own, who specialize in diversions that bring chaos, confusion and destruction within the decision-making of a genuine work of God. They serve as usurpers and then negative conduits of the anointing to redirect the faith and authority of the Kingdom efforts they penetrate. Jesus revealed that: *"they would be known by their fruit."*

Another undermining application of enemy-employed veils is a perversion of the principle of prayer agreement. An embarrassingly large proportion of the enemy's power today is the result of a usurping of the anointing from misguided believers. The deception involves being *blinded by soul issues* and participating in active "agreement" (according to Matthew 18:19) in both word and prayer with *reckless judgments* against members or groups from within the household of faith. It is the devil who serves as the accuser of the brethren. Jesus released the woman caught in adultery by telling her that He did not condemn her, but to *"go and sin no more."* Premature judgment and agreement with the accuser releases division, destruction and unnecessary backlash. If allowed to enlarge and continue, it potentially can wreak havoc with genuine moves of God.

The fractionalization caused by veils of *religious traditions and myths* undermine the unity born of the Spirit. Jesus took a hard stand against the precepts of men, the fruit of which weakens the simple faith required for moves of the Spirit.

Facing Spiritual Reality

Change begins when the veil is correctly discerned and spiritual reality is faced. Only a remnant is needed to rise above the frays and distortions of truth that immobilize and hold us back. It only takes a remnant to act in faith to penetrate the veils that mask and undermine the transforming power of God and confront the evil of this day. Israel's Messianic Jewish community has been just that kind of remnant, paving the way to release transformation in the Land of Promise. It was Daniel, during the Babylonian captivity, who spiritually began the turning of the captivity. It was likewise the faith of Nehemiah whose prayers began mobilizing the restoration needed for his day.

Facing spiritual reality involves recognizing and confronting the lies. It will entail discerning the difference between the enmeshed precepts of misguided religious and overt occult conventions; with *the need to genuinely hear the voice of the Lord.* Intellectual religion that shuns the Spirit and power of God is vulnerable to the seducing tactics of the enemy's propositions. Wherever a significant move of God is underway, there will be counterfeits and diversions.

Quieting the Soul. Facing spiritual reality means getting beyond our soul issues, as well as our sacred spiritual crutches and precepts to allow the pure input of the Holy Spirit. Only then will we be released to operate with the unwavering faith needed to embrace and execute the will of God. Spiritual activity can mount to frenzied levels. Yet, one of the most frequent statements made by the Lord during His earthly ministry was *"fear not!"* Jesus always removes the barriers with which religion has complicated the pathway to God. In an article from Israel's HaAretz (July 31, 2006), a young Jewish IDF medic facing the conflict in Lebanon was quoted as saying: *"I want time to pray before going into battle. Not many of us are religious, but most of the guys believe."*

Sometimes, like James and John, our misguided zeal, premature judgments and limited vision cause us to make things more complicated and miss the simplicity of the big picture. Faith in God is the potency needed to overcome fear and release the power of God that defies the odds. It is that simple faith that will lead this Israeli medic and many others like him into the reality of knowing His Jewish Messiah. It is the quieting of the soul before God that will clear the confusion to discern accurately the spiritual realities around us.

Walking into the Fire. Facing spiritual realities may require us to walk into the fire. The peace or "shalom" outlined in the Bible is not the absence of conflict. It is the result of that alignment or completeness that comes from doing God's will. Confronting evil and reversing its damage may require sacrificing our comfort zones; or even taking a stand that requires risking it all. Shadrach, Meshach, and Abed-Nego refused to compromise. Yet they met the Son of God in the flames of Nebuchadnezzar's furnace and emerged without the smell of smoke. (Daniel 3:15-18) Walking into the fire involves a choice. The choice is to respond in faith or to respond in fear.

Combined Anointings. The days upon us are evil. Few who are confronting the realities of this hour are able to pave a lone pathway. We need new strategies and we desperately need one another. The turbulence and intensity of the battle is calling for a release of the power of God resulting from the Body functioning in unity. This release is maximized by the advantage of *combined anointings*. Yet, the potential impact of combined anointings is tied to overcoming the operational hurdle of *"pointing the finger in scorn"* at the splinters seen in the eyes of members of the Body outside our preferred in-groups.

Combined anointings represent the right spiritual chemistry mixture directed toward a common purpose that creates the synergy that breaks strongholds. Revival releases combined anointings and vice versa. What happens with revival is that barriers are broken down and there is a pure flow of God's Spirit among those operating together. Birds of a feather and loyalty are all nice to have when working together, but unfortunately within the Body, "in-group" standards can become so restrictive and in-bred that they squeeze out spontaneity and innovation and even the anointing. Our boundaries need to be extended.

This is a time when the Lord is putting together unusual alliances between ministries; between businesses and ministries; as well as between businesses, governmental entities and ministries. Collaborative efforts reflecting combined anointings will bring significant results that far surpass the natural. Combined anointings involve much more than gathering for group prayer. It is much more than the type of synergy when two and two make five. It involves a strategic convergence of diverse segments of the Body joining together and actuating results on a level of one and one making a hundred and one.

Emerging Beyond Human Effort

Today's challenges and conflicts are requiring decisions, plans and strategies that go beyond the human effort of even the most talented from our ranks. The societal transformation set in motion by Jesus' followers was led by everyday people simply willing *to believe, obey and take action* with strategies based not on the precepts and traditions of men, but on the basic truths of His Word and on hearing the voice of the Lord. It involves knowing what to do so that the efforts are beyond the arena of the best that human effort might employ. That will involve the combined interaction of an identity totally tied to God, Kingdom truths and dominion.

Identity Issue. The church's job is to perfect the saints for the work of ministry; to equip and mobilize the saints as they grasp and move into the fullness of their callings. That begins with settling the identity issue: of who we are in Him and what we are here to do. Joseph's identity-in-God was recognized and respected by the Egyptians. His faithful stewardship, within that identity, brought honor to the Lord. Becoming secure in our identity and calling of God is a prerequisite to piercing the veil.

Kingdom Truths. The Son of God summed up the wisdom of the Scriptures in the Sermon on the Mount and with a series of parables unveiling Kingdom truths. These truths are paradoxes to the natural mind; yet their application represents gateways into results surpassing the limitations of human effort..

Dominion. Jesus' mission was to destroy the works of the devil and to restore man to the purpose for which God created him; which is the cooperative interaction between God and man to take dominion; to *rule over the works of His hands.*

Piercing the Veil

Not withstanding the God-ordained veils that need to ripen into maturity; piercing demon set veils begins with facing spiritual realities in the power and presence of God. That will involve progressive revelation, consecration and spiritual saturation.

From the days of Adam, Noah, Abraham, David and the prophets; to the days of Jesus and the early Church, the key differentiating factor between the religions of the world and the God of Abraham, Isaac and Jacob, the God of our Lord Jesus has been that God speaks and interacts with His people.

"Hearing the voice of the Lord" involves learning to recognize and correctly *discerning God's guidance* as it is unveiled through His Word, through wisdom and through revelation. In the same way that Peter admonished us to wash ourselves in the truths of God's Word, we also need to bathe the revelation we receive in prayer. Our spiritual receptors mature with use over time. Likewise, the depths of the wisdom of God are such that initial words of guidance received from the Holy Spirit are just that. They are preliminary and in most instances, the framework for receiving the next level of revelation. *Revelation typically comes progressively* in layers, as we diligently seek Him and mature in our ability to correctly discern between soul and Spirit.

Genuine consecration releases authority and the supernatural. Consecration combines prayer, humility and judging yourself before the Lord. Jesus said, *judge yourselves that you be not judged.* It is an examination of the human effort, so that we might yield ourselves more fully to the divine effort. Consecration is a conscious process of spiritually purifying ourselves for the purpose of operating to a greater degree in oneness with the Lord.

Consecration will involve the removal of the beams of our own eyes that create schisms within the Body; avoidance of "evil-speaking" and premature judgments of members of the Body not of our ilk; eliminating the rumor-mill or hearsay as a means of input in the decision-process; averting the orientation toward pat formulas that undermine the wisdom and revelation that are available for specific situations; and removing the infiltrators from within Kingdom decision circles whose impact demonstrate chaos, confusion and reversals.

Consecration will entail spiritual saturation. Spiritual saturation will result from active spiritual maintenance, by effectively employing His Word and the prayer needed to overcome the odds. It involves immersing yourself in God's Word and disciplining yourself to enter that place that Paul spoke of as *"praying without ceasing."* It is an alignment process. With the alignment will come the release of God's intervention.

"By His Spirit He adorned the heavens; His hand pierced the fleeing serpent. These are but the mere edges of His ways, and how small a whisper we hear of Him! But the thunder of His power, who can understand?" Job 26:13-14

The issue for the times upon us is in knowing what to do. The scripture in Luke 9 tells us that Jesus had set his face toward Jerusalem. Yet, in this process, the Samaritans rejected Him. James and John's misguided passion was born of spiritual myopia: to employ the power of God to respond in-kind and bring down judgment on the Samaritans. Jesus knew that the answer to the Samaritans was tied to what would unfold in Jerusalem. James and John responded like zealots, which was contrary to the thrust of the Lord's earthly ministry. Jesus put things back in focus for them — and for us, with the words, *'the Son of Man came not to destroy men's lives, but to save them.'*

Piercing the veil that empowered the transformational move of God described in the book of Acts came with the outpouring of the Holy Spirit. It followed one of history's most brutal times of waiting on God. The cost was paid at the cross. The release came at the resurrection, but the veil was pierced for the believers at Pentecost. It remains the model for this day. It was the veil-piercing that broke the bonds; that constrained the followers of Jesus — then and now, of their misguided zeal, premature judgments and all the other limitations to our best human efforts.

Our impact will mount as we prepare ourselves, as a Body. As we learn to accurately discern the veil, and in faith face the spiritual realties beyond our limitations; we will sharpen our alignment with the Spirit of the Lord and emerge beyond our good intentions and zealous human effort with the power of God to traverse the change and pierce the veils.

"You've not passed this way before, so consecrate yourselves, for the Lord is going to do wonders among you." Joshua 3:4, 5

CHAPTER 21

PREVAILING

"And I will make you to these people as a fortified wall of bronze; they may fight against you, but they will not prevail over you, for I am with you to save and deliver you, says the Lord." Jeremiah 5:22

Prevailing, as one called by God, is a two-edged sword. On the one hand, it represents the adversary's aim when oppressing us. It is the intent of the evil arrayed against us to defeat and destroy what God has called us to do. On the other hand, it is the place of overcoming, of breaking through and gaining genuine ascendancy over the forces coming against us — and of establishing God's authority and rule in our individual spheres.

The realities and response to operating in Egypt and Babylon, with the Chaldean wellspring of sorcery in the wings, were incorporated in the lives of Joseph and Daniel who, against all odds and opposition, changed the course of world events in their day. Joseph and Daniel were each models of people-of-God who had every temptation to "be like everyone else" thrown at them. Then, having prevailing to the point of their promotions, they easily could have been enticed to resign themselves to the "comforts" and conclude the blessings were designed as a "reward" for them.

Yet, neither Joseph nor Daniel diverted from the progressive purposes that God had for their lives. Why? It was because they had conditioned themselves to listen and hear His voice. They each operated at very high levels of prophetic wisdom in their assignments in the midst of the world. Their callings were recognized as being from God by the people of Egypt and Babylon; while simultaneously reflecting the personal standard in Proverbs 16 indicating: *"that he who rules his own spirit is mightier than he who takes a city."*

There likewise is no question that dominion — the authority they needed to operate in as faithful ambassadors of the Lord AND to overcome— involved strong confrontations with the forces of darkness. They refused to back off or compromise. The result was that each prevailed and saw God's authority established in the midst of the most unlikely domains of Egypt and Babylon.

The extremely subtle bottom line of this dynamic of prevailing, for those called as modern-day Josephs and Daniels; those called as facilitators in the infrastructures of what we tend to view as the "world's" systems, is that it is not what we can do for God; but rather what we allow Him to do through us.

The Lord Jesus said: that *"many are called, but few are chosen."* The distinction of being counted among those who are chosen is not according to our standards of achievement and success, but rather to our response to the progressive revelation of operating in obedience as genuine instruments of God's purpose. It is a distinction marked by those who prevail.

As we are poised at His throne and extend ourselves as living sacrifices before Him, let us glean from the wisdom needed to prevail: from the gateway, to the process, while traversing the pathway, to embracing the principles and strategies while understanding the purpose — so that we might enter the place that results from prevailing.

The Gateway to Prevailing

"The Son can do nothing by himself; he can do only what he sees his Father doing, because whatever the Father does the Son also does. For the Father loves the Son and shows him all he does." John 5:19-20

The gateway to prevailing is twofold. It involves a spiritual walk in which our lives are in such oneness with Him that there is not one vestige of variation between our will and His. As that dynamic becomes the mode, we begin gaining entrance into a dimension described by the Apostle Paul, in his second letter to the Corinthians, as being *"beyond human effort."*

The gateway passage punctuates the point already made that it is not what we can do for God; but rather what we allow Him to do through us. It serves as the starting point for those called into transformational roles through business and government. It is the combination of those Kingdom dynamics that reflect strength by yielding; leadership by serving; and authority through humility.

The Process of Prevailing

"He who rules his own spirit is mightier than he who takes a city." Proverbs 16:32

As a former military man, I have an appreciation for and have always been amazed at what this proverb implies. Taking a city involves a significant undertaking. It has to be strategically planned out, with an acute awareness of the obstacles to be encountered at each stage of the assault. It involves operating with an overcoming force that successfully penetrates the defenses of the domain to be surmounted. It entails a unity of effort and concentration of forces that is focused and alert to contingencies in need of tactical response. It also involves a steadfast resolve that doesn't quit until the mission is accomplished.

In light of all that, this proverb says that the one who rules his own spirit is mightier than the one who orchestrates taking a city. Yet again, it is not what we can do for God; but rather what we allow Him to do through us that will be the mark of the process of the one who prevails.

The Pathway to Prevailing

"A man's gift makes room for him and brings him before great men." Proverbs 18:16

Scripture indicates that God gives gifts to men. The Apostle Paul notes: first the natural, then the spiritual. Identifying the natural gift we are each endowed with, but not stopping before identifying and melding it to our unique spiritual gift will become the basis for a community dynamic that is extremely powerful in terms of our roles in advancing the Kingdom of God.

Advancing His Kingdom and operating as community builders are two significant functions that, like the natural and spiritual gifts that operate together, must function in concert with each other. So the pathway to prevailing will involve combining our natural and spiritual gifts so that we begin breaking out of the mold of our old wineskins and worldviews, while embracing the mind-sets that bear on enhancing our unique roles in advancing His Kingdom as community builders.

The new mind-sets that bear most significantly on advancing God's Kingdom are a God-centered, Kingdom mind-set; a Hebraic mind-set; an entrepreneurial mind-set; and a community-centered mind-set.

The application of the Kingdom principles imparted by Jesus to the operation of community will bring transformation. Likewise, embracing a biblical, Hebraic orientation is not simply a step in this process, but is foundational to overcoming the points of stumbling that have plagued the Church for centuries. Similarly, applying entrepreneurial principles rather than the Western institutional ones to not only economic community development, but to relationships and management styles will fuel revival and be the catalyst for transformation. Then, release will come as we put into action the dynamic activated by community representing the repository of gifts that combine to create the synergies that multiply our individual efforts.

The Catalyst for Prevailing

"That we might know the hope of His calling and the riches of His glory." Eph 1:18

Within the pathway are catalysts to the prevailing process. The application of servant leadership and tz'dakah are key catalysts that will bring balance to and fuel the integration of the spiritual, community and economic riches outlined in God's Word. Each has its foundation in humility, the result of which will yield the hope of our callings. We lead by serving and gain by giving. Again, being drawn from Kingdom principles, to the natural man they come across as paradoxes.

Jesus admonished us not to be like the Gentile rulers who like to wield their authority and lord over people. He said that those who are greatest among us should become the least and the leader as a servant.

The community dynamic of tz'dakah insures no one is ever left behind or overlooked. It involves giving, but doing so with purpose and dignity. In Jewish tradition, the highest form of tz'dakah is helping someone to start a business. It is righteousness and charity inexorably intertwined.

The Strategy of Prevailing

"We have this treasure in earthen vessels that the excellence of the power may be of God and not us." 2 Corinthians 4:7

The strategy of prevailing involves an out-of-the-box orientation that is marked by operating beyond human effort. It is that dependency on the supernatural as both the equalizer and the expectation of our callings and efforts tied to our roles as community builders. It has been said that believers ought to be natural in the supernatural and supernatural in the natural. That balance between the natural and supernatural reflects the mode that both Joseph and Daniel operated in.

Prevailing involves a need to break the mold in terms of embracing the opportunities to bring the Lord into the equation—not in terms of precepts, but from the stance of "demonstrating the reality of the Lord operating in our midst." Genesis 39 tells us that "everyone" saw that the Lord was with Joseph and made all that he did to prosper. Likewise, it was seen of Daniel that he reflected ten times the level of wisdom than that of the others serving in the King's court.

The Result of Prevailing

"What is man that You take thought of him, and the son of man that You care for him? Yet, You have made him a little lower than God, and You crown him with glory and majesty! You make him to rule over the works of Your hands." Psalms 8:4-6 NASU

The result from prevailing is dominion. Dominion is the establishment of God's Kingdom rule. It is simultaneously an individual and a community dynamic that evolve when God's Kingdom rule prevails in us and in our domains. It is the economic, community and spiritual penetration of society that draws others to God by the impartation of Life.

In a word, it is the demonstration of the reality of God operating in our midst that will be recognized by those outside the community of believers.

The result is foundational to societal transformation. While the dynamic of prevailing operates on an individual basis, much greater significance will result when it manifests to operate in community, as a Body.

The God-centered, entrepreneurial communities, modeled by Abraham, Isaac and Jacob, give us a snapshot of this dynamic. The Moravians followed it after their renewal during the 1700s.

Then several years ago, I became acquainted with two believers, one being a successful entrepreneur and the other a seasoned community builder, who had formed an alliance to embrace this biblical pattern. They had banded together to mobilize a handful of Christians in an impoverished Buddhist village in rural Southeast Asia. Local gardening was retarded due to the high clay content of the soil and work was scarce. The majority in this village had barely enough to feed their families one meal a day. These pioneers recognized that this was not God's design. The scriptural result from the merging of the spiritual, economic and community dimensions of God's blessings has always been to make God's people to be the head and not the tail.

So, it was after praying about the dilemma faced by this village that an idea crystallized. With an ample supply of clay from the surrounding soil, this remnant of believers turned the curse into a blessing by launching a simple business that created decorative clay pots, designed as wall-hangers. Distribution was found through Western gift shops.

The demand for these clay pots began increasing and soon this handful of Southeast Asian Christians began hiring others from their village as their business expanded. As this enterprise grew, more families were eating two and then three meals a day, as the owners shared with their workers the truths of God's love and His Word. Over time the result was that as hunger was alleviated, the entire village saw the reality of God operating in their midst and fully embraced the goodness and joy of the Lord.

Prevailing as Pioneers

"Let us press on toward the mark of the high call that is in Christ Jesus." Phil 3:14

Many are called, but few are chosen. Prevailing is far more than refusing to give up, although steadfastness is certainly involved. Prevailing has a central focus of entering by the narrow gate spoken of by Jesus, but also of maintaining the pathway that conforms to the higher dimensions of His purposes. Not withstanding the tactical interim battles in the face-off of oppression, prevailing is the long-term, strategic pioneering spirit that comes from God that causes us to operate outside the box of our comfort zones and worldviews.

It is the orientation that is driven, not by the approval of men and the limitations of our conceptual perceptions of reality, but rather that ongoing quest that thirsts for that "something more" that can only come from flowing in oneness with Him. It is the basis of that high call that has as its prime motivation, the reception and clarity of purpose and goals that comes only from the time being spent with Him. It is the alignment of our hearts with His as we reach out and serve others within the framework of God's heart; the result of which is having our lives come together with the meaning and purpose God intended from the beginning.

SECTION IV:

EMBRACING THE MANDATE

CHAPTER 22

THE MANTLE OF POWER

"From the days of John the Baptist until now the kingdom of heaven suffers violence, and the violent take it by force." Matthew 11:12-13

In the clash between good and evil, the crux pivots on the pursuit and wielding of power.

In its purist form, power is a gift of God. The power from God creates, innovates and builds. It serves to replicate itself and multiply. It is the source of blessing. Yet, since the fall of man, power has undergone debasing perversions.

Without God, the basic nature of man corrupts power. Despite the best of intentions, arrogance defiles the purity of the power created by God. Greed pollutes it. Deceit distorts it. Given full reign, manipulation and charm becomes the seedbed of sorcery. Sorcery releases embedded evil that serves to systematically pervert and undermine the power and authority established by God.

Sorcery is the ultimate counterfeit of God's power. It usurps and tears down. The bottom line evidence of God's power is life. The evidence of the devil's power is death.

The Power to Govern

Over the centuries, the conflict between good and evil has seen shifts in the "governing" power between those holding military, economic and religious rule. As such, government has been defined as the organizational structure through which a ruling unit exercises authority and performs functions usually classified by the distribution of power within it.

One of the most potent Messianic scriptures, Isaiah 9, states that *"the government shall be on his shoulder."* Revelation 3 unveils to a segment of the Church at Thyatira that they will rule over the nations. As the balance in His creation is restored, the expectation is for God's Kingdom rule to manifest through those representing His elect.

This restoration of God's rule and authority has systematically been evident through chosen instruments of His purpose. Noah's obedience to the voice of the Lord showed that God's power would not be mocked. Abraham demonstrated the powerful impact that resulted from believing what God told him, while modeling the elements comprising God-centered governance. The Torah outlined the principles on how to run God-centered entrepreneurial communities.

God's Kingdom Power and Strategy

Jesus announced His earthly ministry with the words: *"The Kingdom of God is at hand."* While training a small and unlikely band to follow His footsteps in demonstrating the principles of the Kingdom and its power; Jesus released the strategy to close the gap in restoring God's authority and rule to the earth.

The opening scripture in Matthew 11 describing the dynamic of power operating since the time of John concludes Jesus' basic teaching on the Kingdom, which was followed by Him imparting power to his disciples and sending them out.

Its context is summed up in Matthew 9 with the Lord demonstrating the first steps of reestablishing God's Kingdom rule, by reversing the bondage of corruption by *"healing every disease and sickness among the people."* At that juncture, Jesus called the disciples together and equipped them with the authority to do what He had been modeling.

"When He had called His twelve disciples to Him, He gave them authority over unclean spirits, to cast them out, and to heal every kind of sickness and disease." Matthew 10:1

Jesus' instructions to His followers were to give first priority to the lost sheep of the house of Israel and then:

"As you go, preach, saying, 'The kingdom of heaven is at hand.' Heal the sick, cleanse the lepers, raise the dead, cast out demons. Freely you have received, freely give." Matthew 10: 7-8

Jesus made it plain to those called, that there would be confrontations and division.

"Behold, I send you out as sheep among wolves. So be wise as serpents and harmless as doves. Be wary of men who will betray you. You will even be brought before governors and kings for My sake, as a testimony to them." Matthew 10:16-18

The Mantle of Kingdom Messengers

For those carrying the message of the Kingdom, Jesus made an amazing statement about those who receive the ones He has sent with His authority:

"He who receives you receives Me, and he who receives Me receives Him who sent Me. He who receives a prophet in the name of a prophet shall receive a prophet's reward. And he who receives a righteous man in the name of a righteous man shall receive a righteous man's reward. And whoever gives one of these little ones a mere cup of cold water in the name of a disciple, I assuredly say to you shall by no means lose his reward." Matthew 10:40-42

In a word, the sequence of steps outlined by Jesus in Matthew's gospel were first to receive His Kingdom transforming power, then to go, preach the Kingdom and reverse the curse that came from the fall of man. Then in staying the course in confronting the opposition and establishing His Kingdom rule, He indicated that those who receive His ambassadors, by embracing the Kingdom message, will receive Him.

The Shift

This portion of scripture continues by saying that when He finished instructing His disciples that He went out to teach and preach in the cities. The cities represented the next step in Jesus' progression of confronting the rulers of darkness. At that point, word came from John the Baptist whose confrontation with the authorities had landed him in prison.

Jesus sent word back to John that, in short, told John to hold steady to his course, that the "shift" of power had begun. Then in commenting on John, Jesus said there was none born among women greater than him, yet whoever was least in the Kingdom was greater than John. That statement was then punctuated by the words:

"From the days of John the Baptist until now the kingdom of heaven suffers violence, and the violent take it by force." Matthew 11:12-13

What Jesus was explaining lies at the heart of being a vessel of God's power. Serving as an instrument of God's power means that evil will attempt violence in its attempts to retain its hold on power. Yet, cracking the stronghold of the bondage of corruption involves the demonstration of God's goodness in the face of evil. The principles of God's Kingdom operate with faith and the Kingdom principles reflecting God's nature: wisdom is derived from simplicity; greatness is founded on humility; leadership comes from service; gain is achieved by giving; we live by dying; order evolves from change. These principles are the foundation of God's transforming power. They embody the mantle of power.

An Application of Kingdom Transformation

Joseph the Patriarch was a model of rightly wielding the mantle of power to launch a pathway for Kingdom transformation. He was called into a most unusual time in history. The world at the time was facing devastation. Joseph's time in Egypt was marked by the words in Genesis 39 that *"the Lord was with Joseph and he was a successful man; and everyone saw that the Lord was with Joseph and made all that he did to prosper."*

These words reflected the time Joseph was a slave in Potiphar's house. Joseph heard God's voice. He walked in humility and served faithfully, with diligence. The blessings and wisdom of God flowed from what Joseph applied himself to doing; and Joseph made clear to those he served that the differentiating factor in him was the God he served. From that, the scripture says that *"everyone saw that the Lord was with Joseph and made all that he did to prosper."* So it is as Jesus revealed:

"He who receives you receives Me, and he who receives Me receives Him who sent Me. He who receives a prophet in the name of a prophet shall receive a prophet's reward. And he who receives a righteous man in the name of a righteous man shall receive a righteous man's reward." Matthew 10:40-41

Despite a culture in which sorcery was freely practiced at the highest levels, in each stage in Joseph's tenure in Egypt, there came a shift releasing God's authority. When he was in Potiphar's house, Potiphar saw the blessings and authority of God operating through Joseph. The result was Potiphar entrusting Joseph with his authority. Although it initially seemed that Joseph being thrown into prison was a setback, the jailer did exactly the same thing. Joseph was given charge over all the prison.

Greatness is born from humility. Leadership comes by serving with faithfulness and diligence. He who loves his life will lose it, but he who holds his life of no account will gain it. Blessing is the response to being cursed. Order evolves from change.

So, the pattern followed when Joseph was sent to Pharaoh. The stronghold of sorcery had to bow at Pharaoh's words: *"Can we find such a man as this, one in whom is the Spirit of God? Inasmuch as God has shown you all this, there is no one as wise and discerning as you are. You shall be over my house and all my people shall be ruled according to your word."* (Genesis 41: 38-39) Pharaoh recognized the mantle of power that operated through Joseph came from God; and in that context, Pharaoh received Joseph.

We currently live in a time in history when the level of lawlessness and depravity reflected by the bondage of corruption are such that the establishment of God's Kingdom rule is going to manifest with greater power than in any other time in recent history. It is going to be evidenced through unexpected Joseph-Pharaoh alliances.

The Stronghold of Embedded Evil

The struggle and the strongholds of our day have sorcery at their source. Sorcery is normally more subtle in its manifestation at governing levels. Yet, at the heart of seats of power perpetuating the bondage of corruption will be embedded evil crafted by sorcery.

The old-Covenant Jezebel was the ultimate example of embedded evil in the place of governance. She undermined and implanted her own agendas into the rule of Ahab. Jezebel became the model of those who tear down and usurp what rightfully belongs to others when through guile, deceit and lies she destroyed Naboth in order for Ahab to yield to his lusts in acquiring Naboth's vineyard. Over time, she diverted the course of Israel by systematically eliminating any threat to her insatiable, perverse seizure of power, until she ran into Elijah.

Ambassadors of Power

God's power operates on the opposite track by reclaiming the dominion that rightfully belongs to God and resetting the course to God's agendas. It involves the influence to penetrate key secular strongholds, not through guile, deceit and manipulation, but those seemingly paradoxical principles of goodness that drive the Kingdom. God's power-shifts manifest more dramatically during unlikely or seemingly impossible circumstances.

So it is that today, a parallel is emerging to Joseph's calling that will impact strategic spheres of influence of our day. Joseph's calling could not have been fulfilled apart from Pharaoh. This unorthodox alliance broke all religious tradition. It was a shift of power actuated by the mantle of power that came from the influence of a most unlikely candidate to create a most unlikely alliance with the ruler with the resources to avert disaster and release Life. It was a strategic alliance that was set in motion when Pharaoh recognized the Spirit of God operating in Joseph and received Joseph by yielding his authority to Joseph for the common good. So it will be for those called as the genuine Josephs of today.

"He who receives you receives Me, and he who receives Me receives Him who sent Me. He who receives a prophet in the name of a prophet shall receive a prophet's reward. And he who receives a righteous man in the name of a righteous man shall receive a righteous man's reward. And whoever gives one of these little ones only a cup of cold water in the name of a disciple, assuredly, I say to you, he shall by no means lose his reward." Matthew 10:40-42

CHAPTER 23

THIS IS THE GENERATION

"Ask of me of things to come concerning My sons; and concerning the work of My hands, command you Me." Isaiah 45:11

This passage in Isaiah aptly sums up the life and impact made by Daniel. He sought the Lord and He answered Him. Daniel was fervent in His role as God's ambassador in a caldron of power fueled by sorcery. He served as the catalyst to the shift restoring God's purposes to His people.

Daniel consistently faced what unfolded before him with a Kingdom mind-set. He knew what to do in the most adverse of situations. His perspective reflected not only God's heart, but God's intentions and the Lord's ways of accomplishing His purposes at the generation-level.

"How great are His signs! And how mighty His wonders! His kingdom is an everlasting kingdom, and His dominion is from generation to generation." Daniel 4:3 Amp

Joseph the patriarch, without wavering at the cost, paved the way to reclaim the plan of God's heritage for his people. It was a heritage that had been all but lost by the indiscretions of the generation represented by his brothers.

Moses was raised up as a deliverer to break the bondage of conformity and lead a generation of God's people into the purposes of God. Yet, due to the short-sidedness of that generation, it would take another generation to enter the place of God's promise and calling.

When it comes to God's redemptive purposes, the Lord works through generations and those He has anointed to lead a generation. For each generation, there is a mantle of opportunity extended.

It is through a generation that the shifts required for God's course corrections are set in motion. When a generation enters and embraces a unity-of-purpose tied to what the Spirit is bringing forth, then amazing things will happen. These amazing things will break the mold and operate against the odds; and God will be glorified not only among His people, but among outsiders witnessing the realities of God operating in their midst.

Understanding the Times

"Till the Spirit is poured out from on high, and the desert becomes a fertile field, and the fertile field seems like a forest, justice will dwell in the desert and righteousness live in the fertile field." Isaiah 32:15-16

Before us is an outpouring of the Spirit that will shake the infrastructures of the world's power systems. The shaking has begun. This shaking has released a shift within the Body globally. Old models appropriate for their time no longer work. It will be a time of awe with a cleansing and removal of dead wood, as in the time of Shebna (Isaiah 22).

The spiritual leadership required during a shift carries a cost that cannot be accomplished by any means other than humility and holiness. The servant leaders at the forefront of this move of the Spirit are ones who will evidence the true operation of the Kingdom paradoxes imparted by Jesus. As this shift aligns, there will be a touching of generations.

The Mantle of Facing Adversity

A generation is emerging to assume the mantle. It is one largely free from the entanglements and limitations of those whose mindsets and approach to the Kingdom have been diluted and tainted by achievement and institutional conformity. It will prove to be a trusted generation, one totally unfazed by the influence of wealth and power.

It is a generation that is not beguiled by the status quo or intimidated by the prospect of change. It understands the most basic premise of business ...that opportunity will yield, as adversity is faced head-on, by managing change. This generation of God's people is poised to pierce the bondage of corruption and move forward with the mind-sets needed to extend and redeem God's purposes across the earth—to its generation.

"Sing aloud to God our strength, for this is a statute for Israel. This He established in Joseph as a testimony, when he went through the land of Egypt. He called in trouble and You delivered him. You answered him in the secret place of thunder." Psalm 81:1-7

For those who rule their own spirits in the fire, God's answers from the crucible of "the secret place of thunder" will change the course of nations.

"The Lord thunders with His majestic voice and does not restrain the lightning when His voice is heard. The Lord thunders wondrously with His voice, doing great things beyond our comprehension." Job 37:4

This generation carries the anointing of the societal-transforming, pioneering leadership modeled by Joseph and Daniel. It is a generation that will follow the pathway navigated by Joshua and Caleb, who took their generation into the land of their calling.

Generational Identity

As the mantle is passed, each generation must stand on the foundation of its own identity in God. Each generation must wield the mantle of its own calling marked by its own unique identity. The generation coming forth reflects the context seen by Daniel many years ago.

"In the time of the end, many shall be purified and refined, but the wicked will do wickedly and none of the wicked will understand, but the wise shall understand." Daniel 12:10

Unlike any generation in recent history, this one will usher in a time of closing the gap between the purposes of God and the power structures of this world. It will find its identity in facing the fire. Yet, the fire of adversity bears no restraint to the one truly addicted to God's presence, as Joseph and Daniel were.

God's presence is a consuming fire. Those entering this time of His strategic purpose must reflect the sanctification required for the calling, in order to avoid being overwhelmed and consumed. Prayer support is essential, but if those called haven't acquired their own authority to match the calling, then regardless of the prayers rendered by others, the effort will fall short.

Spiritual maturity involves piercing the veil by means of the Spirit rather than the flesh. It is the proactive, ongoing encounter with God rather than the vicarious group-think of the information junkie. Beyond connecting the dots and laying foundations, will come the facing of the fire that brings things full circle to closing the gap of the fullness of God's intentions for this generation.

The Gateway to Reality

Reality in its purist sense is spiritual. The Word aptly applied provides the pathway of godliness that guides us into His presence. God is Spirit and they that know Him must know Him in Spirit and in Truth. Spirit controls matter. Without the active revelation that guided Joseph and Daniel into their destinies, our worldview, even our 21st century, western Christian worldview is at best a constraining filter. The truest foundation to viewing reality is in hearing the voice of the Lord.

Hebrews 3 speaks of a generation that made the Lord angry. It was a generation with a worldview that was never quite able to divorce itself from its dependency on Egypt for its identity and purpose. Despite it being a generation that for over forty years saw some of the most remarkable works of God seen by man, as well as being the recipients of the Torah; yet the Word tells us that they failed to know His ways. Most revealing, in this sequence of scripture, is that knowing God's ways had its pivot point on hearing His voice. Again, in the fourth chapter of Hebrews is the same admonition: *"today, if you will hear His voice, do not harden your hearts."*

Throughout the Bible, those who were the heroes of faith were those who knew His ways and discerned the voice of the Lord as if it were the most natural thing in the world. They were the leaders and prophets who knew God's heart and whose efforts were based on a calling to mobilize their generation.

A Mobilized Generation
Over the centuries, God's desire has been for a mobilized generation; a generation who would hear and obey His voice. Jesus broke the mold to the institutional constraints that marked the sad condition of God's people at the time of His coming. Again and again, the Lord Jesus made reference to the generation in which He came. He referred to it as being evil and perverse.

Especially noted among those described this way were the leaders of the religious establishment, who were trapped by intellectualism and full of their own self-importance. They were seduced by power and aligned with whatever it took for their own personal advancement. Rather than serving and facilitating the mobilization of everyday people for God, they had become sowers of hurdles that set their personal nests on high and encumbered the pathway of others in God.

Peter describes the result of what Jesus released, within the context of that generation representing a "nation," mobilized to pave the way from darkness into Light.

"But you are a chosen generation, a royal priesthood, a holy nation, His own special people, that you may proclaim the praises of Him who called you out of darkness into His marvelous light."
1 Peter 2:9

Yet, the spontaneity and fervor of the early Church waned into becoming institutionalized and powerless. While the winds of the Spirit would fan the fire of God in a way that impacted individual generations, the continuity between generations has been largely fragmented until now.

The Heritage of Dominion

Beyond our individual callings is a multi-generational heritage. It is the heritage that restores God's rule and authority—His dominion across the earth. That *"great cloud of witnesses"* referred to in Hebrews 12 a unique, "across-the-ages" glimpse of this multi-generational heritage.

"Bless the LORD, all you His hosts, you ministers of His, who do His pleasure." Psalm 103:21

The restoration of dominion is a heritage that the generations will share. The process that will bring it together, however, is one punctuated at the generational level.

God created man *"to rule over the works of His hands."* That's the basis of what we call dominion. Closing the gap to God's rule and authority will take an unusual, anointed generation to pave the way. Many notable leaders in this last generation have made an impact; yet less than a handful have brought strategic change to its generation. That is what this shift is all about: the alignment that will change the course of a generation.

The Joseph-Daniel Generation

The context involves the penetration of the infrastructures of the world's systems for the restoration of God's dominion. While there have been many forerunners and pioneers, for the most part, the emerging Joseph-Daniel "generation" will be ones assuming their mantles between the ages of their early thirties to mid-forties. It follows the pattern of Jesus, Joseph, Daniel and David, whose exploits for the Lord peaked at these ages.

Not to be confused with the benevolence and impact of the array of those being mobilized in mid-life, which reflects its own unique mantle, the Joseph-Daniel generation will pave new ground from the onset. They will understand the connection between the bottom-up and top-down strategies for transformation. They will work alongside of and be fathers to the Pharaohs in their spheres, with their counsel being heeded for their good. They will turn famine into opportunity.

They will reflect a mix of wisdom and humility that earns the trust and favor of the most scrutinizing. Their decisions and modus operandi will consistently demonstrate the prophetic wisdom and reality of God operating in their midst. Their authority will be tied to enabling opportunity that builds community and with it, the Kingdom.

Their perspectives will be shaped not by contemporaneous worldviews and doctrines, but by the wisdom of God's Word with their spirits being forged in the fire of His presence. Their impact will be marked by the subtle difference between what they can do for God and what they allow God to do through them. They will embrace the solitude required for the continuity of hearing the voice of the Lord, without the enticements of the approval of men. They are ones who the world can trust, who will thrive and bring order out of chaos during times of shaking.

"Blessed is the one who trusts in the Lord. He is like tree planted by the rivers of waters, whose leaves stay green. In the time of drought, he knows no distress, but bears fruit." Jeremiah 17:7

So it is that among us today are those emerging as generation-shakers, leaders who will move on a level that is not just strategic, but bears the imprint of those Kingdom paradoxes and those who, throughout the ages, operated outside the box in the way they heard God's voice. They are a generation who will hear and respond as one …to the heart and voice of the Lord.

"This is the generation of those who seek Him, who seek Your face — even Jacob." Ps 24:6

CHAPTER 24

THE CORPORATE COMMUNITY

These are serious times. Serious times call for something more. In early 1996 I wrote:

"A time is coming soon when there will be changes in the infrastructures of the world's systems that will create reversals resulting in discontinuities such as the world has never seen. In the same manner that Joseph the patriarch was sent ahead to prepare for what was coming to the earth, God is today sending individuals ahead to prepare for a time of great change that will precede the shift of all ages. These will be individuals who clearly hear God's voice and who possess a unique understanding of the times, who will be thrust into positions of influence within the economic, governmental and business infrastructures that guide the course of world events."

A dynamic unique to our times points to the "something more" that is needed. Fifty three of the top one hundred economies in the world are corporations (*Global, Inc.*, Gabel and Bruner, 2003, The New Press, New York).

With a handful of corporate giants controlling most of the world's energy, technology, banks, industry, food, and media, this means there are corporations that function as kingdoms, with amazing resources at their command.

In view of the political, social and economic framework that we unconsciously depend on for our future, this dynamic unlocks a remarkable dimension to understanding the role of this generation's emerging Josephs. It represents an extraordinary potential to navigating through challenging times.

As Egypt served during a time of great famine in the days of Joseph, so there will be economic-community havens immune to the prevailing disruptions. They will be driven by unconventional alliances, not unlike what operated between Pharaoh and Joseph. They will function as communities of refuge and serve overriding Kingdom purposes.

The Corporate Community Model

At turning points to the destiny of God's people, the Lord has appointed oases, places of refuge that facilitate His overriding Kingdom purposes. Select corporations, the size to be an economy, will align with modern-day Josephs and conform to the age-old biblical model of community to become gateways and shelters from the storm.

The secular-Kingdom paradigm between Joseph and Pharaoh is a model for times of change. The combination of righteous influence (hatz'dakah) and the power of self-sustaining enterprise-communities will bring increase and blessing that extend far beyond their own boundaries. They likewise will provide safe-havens for Kingdom pathways in otherwise hostile environments.

What is frequently referred to as the "global community" has embraced its political, economic and social assumptions on a top-down model that has become increasingly isolated from its bottom-up foundations. From an organizational and market stance, this is a source of mounting instability.

The Word of God clearly outlines a bottom-up foundation. When an entity loses touch with its bottom-up foundations, it will begin to wobble. Economically, the imbalance created by an unhealthy top-down focus will eventually destabilize the entire system.

The dynamic of corporate community is key to stability. Stability that stands strong against the destructive forces of change will result from a healthy top-down, bottom-up balance. Entrepreneurship provides that balance. Key elements of God's DNA, to create, innovate, build and bring increase, are at the heart of God's gift of entrepreneurial community. When entrepreneurship and community are rightly aligned and God-centered, they represent the relational and economic balance through which God's blessings are allowed to flow in a societal context.

Many multinational corporations are community-minded, but far too often swayed by politically-correct spheres of influence. The influence needed to navigate the turbulence of our day will come from Joseph-type alliances. When combined with the bottom-up framework of rightly aligned, smaller, self-sufficient support enterprises, then the top-down shelter of corporate community will result.

When it does, it represents the basis for the proactive response to times of famine and change: the "safe havens;" the ability to bypass disaster; and the approach to bring increase and blessing in spite of the adversity.

The Pathway of the Undefiled

There was a reason Joseph was chosen from among his brothers to be sent ahead. Despite his status when a slave and then a prisoner; Joseph's heart was always that of a king. He was undefiled by the iniquities gripping his brothers. What he took to Egypt was a pure heart that heard from God. What the Egyptians saw was a man, who despite the adversity of his situation bestowed the blessings of God on those he served. When Joseph was a slave in Potiphar's household he was described in this way:

"The Lord was with Joseph and he was a successful man; and everyone saw that the Lord was with Joseph and made all that he did to prosper." Genesis 39:2-3

Joseph's pathway to the palace was one of humility, an identity in God, service to the community and excellence. Joseph was one clearly counted among the 'Tzadikim," the righteous who are recognized as making a difference for the community.

This community dynamic of "tz'dakah," charitable righteousness, became the basis on which the granaries became the source of life during the famine, for not only Egypt, but the world around them. In the process it also became the sanctuary for the birthing of the next step for what the Lord intended to do through His chosen people.

Issues for Influence

There is no question that we face a time of preparation as the assumptions guiding the global community teeter. Persecuted segments of the Body can offer great insight into the priorities and strategies that enable God's people to first survive and then find opportunity in times of crisis. Joseph's influence in Egypt progressively reflected the wise combination of key alliances, new mind-sets, trust, resource application and God-anointed leadership.

Alliances. The choice of alliance will always allow God at the center, without promoting religious convention. The God-centered focus will pivot on the practical benefits to those directly involved. Given full reign, this type of alliance will spill over to bless those around it. In short, these are alliances that operate on the basis of community as God intended, with realignments from the hindrances of business as usual.

Mind-Sets. Jesus taught that unless we become as little children, we will by no means enter the Kingdom of God. In addition to humility, children think outside the box. The wonder of life remains such that for most small children, nothing is impossible. Faith begins with our thinking, our mind-sets.

Pathways that may appear as unconventional will challenge prevailing mind-sets. Joseph's alliance with Pharaoh was an unorthodox departure from the way Jacob's community had previously operated with the world around them. So it is that we've entered a time that will separate man's doctrines from God's principles.

Trust. A major factor operating for Joseph was trust. Joseph was no doubt creative and innovative. Yet he was a most unlikely candidate to be entrusted with the level of authority he was given at each stage in his tenure in Egypt. There was more to it than his character or abilities. Joseph earned the trust of the Egyptians by consistently releasing the blessings of God to the benefit of the community around him.

Resources. Community cannot function properly without the self-supporting flow of resources. There existed an antagonistic response to outsiders by both Jacob and Joseph's brothers. While called to be a light shining in the darkness; to be blessed to be a blessing, they fell short. God's extraction to place Joseph in the heart of Egypt was totally out of sync with the prevailing religious mind-sets. Yet, it placed Joseph amid a people with whom he had great favor, along with the resource- and power-base needed for the coming crisis.

Leadership. His God-centered leadership demonstrated a significant part of Joseph's role. Joseph always found the common ground from which God was openly acknowledged and released in his service to the Egyptians. Leadership involves influence and influence is based on trust. True leadership is the ability to turn insight, inspiration and intention into reality without controlling, manipulating, domineering or forcing. At each stage during his time in Egypt, Joseph broke the mold in the way he mobilized people and resources to the benefit of those around him. When the opportunity presented itself, Joseph demonstrated the leadership needed to mobilize the entire community of Egyptians for a time of crisis.

The Corporate Community Mantle

During the middle-ages power rested in the hands of the few. The feudal system of those days was based on a view that the populace were sheep to be herded and then shorn in due season. Three classes of people existed: the nobility or ruling class; the clergy; and the common folk. The nobility were men who had a duty to protect the others; the clergy served to maintain the souls of the members of society; and beneath both were the commoners, whose role it was to labor and by their efforts to feed the others.

Within the world today is a parallel. It thrives on the premise that if given the freedom, most people will imitate someone else. Yet, blind obedience is not the standard for God's people. Contemporizing God's truth to "become like everyone else" will only cycle into falling short. God's intention for His people has long been to make them *"the head rather than the tail."* His purpose for His own is to *"lend to many nations and not borrow."*

The Kingdom of God will not be built apart from community and enterprise. Weathering the winds of change will not happen apart from defining the identity and leadership needed for the corporate community mantle.

Before us are cyclic times that foreshadow great change. Simultaneously the shift underway will unveil gateways to unusual alliances that excel against adversity in the face of the gathering storms.

For us to assume our role as the people of God there is a clarion call for the Joseph-Daniel type of leadership, along with understanding and applying the biblical framework for community. Both pivot on the admonition from Exodus 15 that provides the key to bypass destruction: *"Listen carefully to the voice of the Lord your God and do what is right in His eyes…"* From Noah to Joseph to Moses to David to the first-century believers, each of whom gave birth to the new thing God was doing for their time, the leadership they exhibited pivoted on hearing the voice of the Lord.

So it is today. Leadership will be defined by those who hear. Community will be defined by those who lead. Those who hear and those who lead will restore the age-old biblical foundations and the true identity and calling that we, as God's people, will use to form alliances and extend God's blessings to the staggering world around us.

"Then the kingdoms of this world will become the kingdoms of our Lord and he shall reign for ever." Rev.21: 10

CHAPTER 25

THE MOST HUMBLE

"Curse not the king, no, not even in your thoughts, and curse not the rich in your bedchamber, for a bird of the air will carry the voice, and a winged creature will tell the matter." Eccl 10:20

Scripture tells us that prior to the time of the Exodus, that *"Moses was very great in the land of Egypt, in the sight of Pharaoh's servants and the people."*

Moses was the deliverer of God's people, Israel. Despite his reluctance when God called him, he confronted and prevailed against Pharaoh, probably the most powerful king on the earth in his day. Moses mobilized and led over a million men, women and children. He worked a level of miracles that are still common knowledge throughout the world, despite the passage of centuries and centuries. Moses likewise outlined the revelation of God that has become the modern-day standard for government, law, morality, economics and spirituality.

In a word, Moses reversed the curse against God's people and established God's authority, rule and dominion that has set the course not only for those known by His name, but to the benefit of Western Civilization to this day.

Yet, in Numbers 12:3 it tells us: *"Now the man Moses was very humble, more than all men who were on the face of the earth."*

The one who is humble is unpretentious and devoid of arrogance in behavior, attitude and spirit. The humble person is outer-directed, with little evidence of the self-absorbed patterns we too often observe among those wielding the trappings of what the world considers success.

On the surface, this statement of Moses being more humble than all men on the face of the earth seems to contradict the mode of one who has made such an impact on history. Yet, it bears the true mark of a Kingdom leader. Unfortunately, this element of leadership is the very point of stumbling for those who otherwise, might be chosen to be among "the great" in the Kingdom.

The Human Point of View

The context for this scripture describing Moses' humility was when his inner circle reduced the call of God on Moses' life to a human point of view.

"Then Miriam and Aaron spoke against Moses ... and the LORD heard it." Num 12:1

Not only did *"the Lord hear it;"* but when it happened, He intervened to draw the line. This sequence of scripture goes on to say that the anger of the Lord was aroused against Moses' older brother and sister.

"Suddenly the LORD said to Moses, Aaron, and Miriam, 'Come out, you three, to the tabernacle of meeting!' Then the LORD came down in the pillar of cloud and stood in the door of the tabernacle, and called Aaron and Miriam. And they both went forward. Then He said, 'Hear now My words: If there is a prophet among you, I, the LORD, make Myself known to him in a vision; I speak to him in a dream. Not so with My servant Moses; he is faithful in all My house. I speak with him face to face, even plainly, and not in dark sayings. Why then were you not afraid to speak against My servant Moses?'" Num 12: 2-8

As Moses' inner circle, Aaron and Miriam wielded great influence among the Israelites. Aaron was Moses' right-hand man who served as priest over the people. Miriam was Moses' sister who had rescued Moses as a baby. Considered a prophetess, she was known best for leading the women in a song of triumph after the passage through the Red Sea.

Why God's Sovereign Intervention

Why did the Lord intervene so suddenly, in such a sovereign and dramatic way?

First, there was not one vestige of variation between God's will for His people and the outworking of the call of God on Moses. When Jesus revealed our accountability for "idle words," it was due to the influence and destructive nature words can have to impede and even derail agendas set in motion by the Lord. Moses' inner circle's words, spoken in whispers, had an impact on his spirit…and on the people.

"Curse not the king, no, not even in your thoughts, and curse not the rich in your bedchamber, for a bird of the air will carry the voice, and a winged creature will tell the matter." Eccl 10:20

Likewise, the timing of this encounter was significant. It was just prior to Moses sending the spies into Canaan. Miriam and Aaron's short-sided yielding to their own agendas and personal ambition brought into question Moses' calling and authority. The second verse of Numbers 12 reads:

"So they said, 'Has the LORD indeed spoken only through Moses? Has He not spoken through us also?'"

So, the Lord heard it. Miriam was struck with leprosy. Aaron immediately repented and begged Moses to heal her. Moses prayed for his sister. The Lord then gave instruction for Miriam to be shamed for all to see …and put outside the camp for seven days, before being healed and allowed back.

God's intervention was revealing. This was not a struggle for power. Both Aaron and Miriam were already a part of the authority structure in leading the Israelites. It was an issue tied to the significance of Moses' calling, of what the Lord was setting in motion through him, and the influence his siblings' words had on the situation. In the midst of a world of lawless, ungodly, oppressive feudal systems, the Lord, through Moses, was setting in motion change ...a God-centered economic governmental template not only for His people, but as a light for the nations to see for the generations to come.

God heard it and intervened. Because of their position of leadership, Aaron and Miriam's words held potential to sway their generation. Moses, as an apostolic prophet was called to change the course of history. The Lord intervened to prevent their steps digressing into matters of ego and ambition.

"The secret things belong to the Lord, but those that are revealed belong to us and to our children forever." Deut 29:29

The Standard for Leadership

Moses is the universal model for God-centered leadership. The mix between his capability, authority and humility represents the standard for priestly kings called to the arena of economic community leadership.

Despite being raised to ascend to the court of Pharaoh, Moses never took himself seriously. As deliverer of God's people, he was intensely purposeful about his calling. His calling fit within the context of a father's heart for his people ...with the authority and direction he wielded coming from God's presence. Within his calling, it was not about him. Moses exhibited no personal ambition. He was paving new ground. With the exception of failing to speak to the rock, Moses restrained himself from yielding to a "self" orientation and the insecurities so often reflected by ones groomed to sit in high places.

The catalyst undergirding his leadership was the ongoing priority Moses gave to spending time in God's presence. It is the time that inoculates God's leaders from the seductive issues of ambition and ego and man-pleasing influences that come from being in the limelight.

The Moses Leadership Distinctive

"Now the man Moses was very humble, more than all men who were on the face of the earth." Num 12:3

The distinction between Moses and his siblings was significant. Miriam was driven by ambition and ego, while Aaron was a man-pleaser. Both orientations are stumbling blocks to being fully used as an instrument of God's purpose. Ambition, ego and a man-pleasing spirit likewise undermine the authority and level at which an intercessor can wield transformational prayers. They each bog down and undermine genuine leadership, authority and the accomplishment of God's true agendas.

Despite Moses being considered very great in the land, being "great" did not happen to be something Moses sought to touch. His leadership was not the result of ambition, ego or his grooming to be a prince in Egypt. "Kingdom success" bears a very different definition than palace success. Moses' time in the presence of the Lord reshaped his perspective and made clear the tasks of his calling. His leadership reflected the balance between serving the people entrusted to his care and the eternal purpose God was releasing through them.

"Let this mind be in you which was also in Christ Jesus, who, being in the form of God, did not consider it robbery to be equal with God, but made Himself of no reputation, taking the form of a bondservant, and coming in the likeness of men. And being found in appearance as a man, He humbled Himself and became obedient to the point of death, even the death of the cross." Phil 2:5-8

The Balance

Moses was exceptionally generous in giving of himself to the people; yet was unrelenting in yielding himself to God. One without the other will fall short of a high calling ...and that of a Kingdom leader.

Moses reflected the heart of a true leader, as well as intercessor. His focus was uniquely balanced between the tension of advancing God's agendas and caring for and guiding His people. He placed the destiny of his people before his own.

"Then Moses returned to the LORD and said, 'Oh, these people have committed a great sin, and have made for themselves a god of gold! Yet now, if You will forgive their sin — but if not, I pray, blot me out of Your book which You have written.'" Ex 32:31-32

The Mark of the Calling

The Cost. The mark of the calling begins with the cost paid for it. Jesus said: *"many are called but few are chosen."* The call of God is not a matter of merit, achievement or recognition. Nor is it a character-development program. God's calling is a unique alignment between the one called and the Lord …that manifests in dominion. It releases life, establishes God authority and brings the change that sets things in order. It advances God's Kingdom by enabling God's people. The call of God, as the Lord intends it, will never materialize without paying the cost.

"By faith Moses, when he had grown to maturity and become great, refused to be called the son of Pharaoh's daughter, preferring to share the oppression and bear the shame of the people of God rather than to have the fleeting pleasures of sin. He considered the contempt and abuse and shame borne for the Messiah Who was to come to be greater wealth than all the treasures of Egypt, for he looked ahead to his reward. By faith he left Egypt behind him, being unawed and undismayed by the wrath of the king; for he never flinched but held staunchly to his purpose and endured steadfastly as one who gazed on Him Who is invisible." Heb 11:24-27 Amp

Believers in the developing world have a much better grasp of the cost of the calling than those of us in the West.

"Let no person trouble me by making it necessary for me to vindicate my apostolic authority and the divine truth of my Gospel, for I bear on my body the brand marks of the Lord Jesus, the wounds, scars, and other outward evidence of persecutions — these testify to His ownership of me!" Gal 6:17 Amp

Hearing His Voice. Moses was consumed by his need to spend time in the presence of the Lord. As a prince in Egypt, he knew of his heritage as an Israelite and no doubt had been made aware of his calling. The many years that followed his misfire of *"wanting to do something,"* when he killed the oppressive Egyptian guard, progressed and resulted in his dramatic encounter with God. That encounter set the stage for every step he took from that point on. Hearing God's voice became Moses' foremost priority. It was the basis of his zeal, wisdom, anointing, authority and decision-making that would influence the generations to come.

"*So the Lord spoke to Moses face-to-face, as a man speaks to his friend.*" Exodus 33:11

Faithful in All of God's House. "*Faithful in all of God's house*" is the word the Lord used to describe Moses when confronting Aaron and Miriam. Moses' calling was a transformational calling that would provide the seedbed that restored God's pathway for future generations. It planted a stake for the shift best described in the Bible by the word dominion. It suggests a comprehensive oneness of heart between the Lord and Moses. It reflects Moses' grasp of the strategic, eternal nature of God's intentions and plans.

"*For creation longs for the revealing of the sons of God …that it might be delivered from the bondage of corruption...*" Rom 8:19-21

True intercessors link the heart, and as such the will of God, with the heart of the people. It's what Ezekiel spoke about by standing in the gap. Moses was as totally in touch with God's heart, as he was with the people's heart. He had the wisdom to know the balance of his responsibility between the two.

Yielded to Him. Whether fat or fragile, issues of ego yield the same result. They undermine and cause high callings to fall short. God will never intervene, as He did for Moses, for the ambitious or for agendas driven by ego or a man-pleasing spirit. Moses was called to change the course of history. In doing so, he was yielded to and one with the Lord.

Being truly yielded to God will bear the mark of humility: of being unpretentious and devoid of arrogance in behavior, attitude and spirit. The humble person is outer-directed, with little evidence of the focus on self and the identity issues that seem to follow what the world considers success.

Jesus said: "*he who loses his life for my sake will find it.*" The humble are those who no longer view their lives or the agendas entrusted to them from a human point of view. They are sold out and aligned with Him. It defines the difference between those who attempt "to do" something for God, and those who allow the Lord to truly operate His will through them.

"So the first shall be last and the last first. For many are called, but few are chosen." Matt 20:16

CHAPTER 26

THE DIVIDING ASUNDER

"Enter by the narrow gate; for wide is the gate and broad is the way that leads to destruction and many are those who go in by it. But narrow is the gate and difficult is the way which leads to life, and there are few who find it." Matthew 7:13

The King James translation of Hebrews 4:12 refers to the "dividing asunder." "Asunder" is the place of key distinction between different parts. The "dividing asunder" is where those distinctions are blurred and veiled. Since the days of Adam and Eve, the evil one has sought to mask key distinctions between soul and spirit.

The times have become uncertain. Nations, cultures and communities have been subjected to wide swings of change. People are looking for answers. People want to be enlightened. Yet, historically the search for enlightenment has instead more often produced masks over what should be spiritual distinctions.

The Enlightenment Illusion

Black has been called white and white black; evil has been called good and good evil, with the resulting contagion referred to as enlightenment. In the early twentieth century the "enlightened" were liberated from personal responsibility when Freud's spin on psychology became the rage, blaming ones' shortfalls on their upbringing and adherence to chaste mores. Its precepts released a subtle force undermining the virtue upheld by the culture at that time.

Jesus pulled back the veil of confusion that masked the pathway into true enlightenment. Introducing His earthly ministry with the words, *"the Kingdom of God is at hand,"* He prepared His disciples to enter by a different dimension. It was the gateway to restore God's original mandate for His people to rule over the work of His hands. It was the narrow path to releasing His Kingdom *"on earth, as it is in heaven."*

Paul began his letter to the Romans by applauding them for their faith. He noted that their faith was being spoken of throughout the world. In that same sequence Paul mentioned the mutual faith he shared with them. Yet, in verse eleven he expressed his desire to impart *"a spiritual gift to them, that they might be established."* Then in the fifteenth verse, he tells them that he was *"ready to preach the gospel to them."*

Paul was unmasking the dividing asunder between those who believe and those whose faith will make a difference. His reference to *"preaching the gospel to them"* was to the Kingdom distinction that would establish the Romans in the destiny entrusted to every believer to "turn the world upside down" (Acts 17: 6).

The Fine Line

The dividing asunder: it's the fine line faced by all believers in making a difference by establishing God's Kingdom rule. It's the distinction between the gospel of salvation and the gospel of the Kingdom. It's the fork in the pathway between the impact made by the good intentions of the soul and the perfect result of the Spirit. It's the difference between having your ears tickled and paying the cost of a high calling. It's the reality-of-God needed to restore godliness in a world seeking the secular enlightenment that has minimized the power in God's people, as the pathway of destruction has been widened.

The masks that have blurred soul and spirit have created potent spiritual counterfeits, counterfeits of destruction that have added to the very turbulence people have sought to avoid. Paul's opening words to the Romans goes on to refer to those who suppress the truth in ungodliness and unrighteousness.

The Key Distinction

Jesus said that it would be by knowing the truth that we would be set free. Yet today even those, like Paul was writing to in Rome, who we share a mutual faith with, have need of an "impartation of a spiritual gift, that they might be established." They need the gospel, the full Gospel, preached to them. When Jesus referred to the gospel it was to the gospel of the Kingdom, which restores the original purpose God had for His people: to rule over the work of His hands.

The truth Jesus imparted, that would set us free, involves reestablishing God's authority. It is what the Scripture refers to as dominion, the mandate for God's Kingdom rule. It bears on the dividing asunder between soul and spirit.

Dominion, the foundation for God's Kingdom rule, is what is lacking in the quest for enlightenment among believers whose sights have been limited to conforming to the standards of those around them. It's the blurring of the spiritual realities resulting in believers whose aim is to become like the world around them. In so doing, they quench the Spirit's power and potential to bear world-changing fruit.

Kingdom Identity

Jesus said to: *"seek first the Kingdom of God and His righteousness."* In short, we muddy the pathway, by going head to head with the world around us, when we hold the Kingdom advantage and the Spirit. Proverbs 3:5 tells us that in trusting the Lord, not to lean unto our own understanding. Walking in the Spirit is an entirely different dimension. It's where it all begins. It's beyond our limited understanding. It's the catalyst to true enlightenment.

"It is the Spirit who gives Life. Human effort accomplishes nothing. And the very words I have spoken to you are spirit and life." John 6:63 NLT

Every believer is given a measure of faith. To what end that faith is applied is the distinction Paul was making. Until we truly yield ourselves to be vessels of His purpose and bridge that dividing asunder, we will remain spiritually anemic and stuck between soul and spirit. It was what distinguished Joseph in the eyes of the Egyptians around him, as the scripture describes him in Potiphar's house.

"The Lord was with Joseph and he was a successful man; and everyone saw that the Lord was with Joseph and made all that he did to prosper." Genesis 39: 2-3

Paul went on to explain to the Romans about the most basic spiritual gifts, by which their pathway would be established; gifts that would distinguish them and their efforts from everyone else.

"So it depends not on human will or exertion, but on God who shows mercy." Rom 9:16 NRSV

The Dividing Asunder of Culture

The blurring of the arena of culture has been diabolically subtle. By penetrating and establishing itself in societal cultures, the kingdom of darkness has confused the genuine cultural identities of unique social groups with the standards of destruction that become known as "the world." This is the reason Paul admonished the Romans not to be conformed to this world, but to be transformed by the renewing of their minds, that they may *prove what is that good and acceptable and perfect will of God.* Romans 12:2 NKJV

Paul was unveiling the steps needed to become established and reach for that perfect will of God. In that same sequence, he outlined seven key gifts whose unique operation in each believer would determine not only their individual identities and callings in the Lord, but the distinction they would embrace as a people in a world gone amok.

The Heart of Darkness

Rome spiritually represented the seat of power of the world of its day. It was the heart of darkness in the struggle between soul and spirit. Its significance in Paul's day should awaken us to the distinctions that, like Joseph the patriarch, we might establish God's Kingdom rule and bring transformation to the seats of power in the world around us.

Paul, schooled in Jewish tradition spent the first three years after his conversion in the desert communing with the Spirit of the Lord. The resulting revelations gave clarity to the distinctions that had been blurred in the covenant calling of the Jewish people. Paul then went on to plant the seeds of transformation in the Gentile world that was described in Acts 17 with the words: *"these who have turned the world upside down have come here too!"*

Yet, here the church is in the 21st century; building buildings and creating programs of relevance that attract new members while the world sets both the standard and the pathway to which we conform. We seem blind to see the distinction beyond an identity of a higher level of ethics and of being such nice people.

That which once pierced the impossible with the possible is explained by human reasoning. The prospect of the ordinary becoming the extraordinary is swallowed up by those seeking to be like everyone else.

Crossing the Threshold

Entering the narrow path Jesus spoke of represents both the start and the challenge. The gateway into God's Kingdom is narrow, indeed. Yet, it serves to form the very distinction that bridges the natural with the supernatural, naturally. It leads in a pathway that consists of the power of God that changes nations.

In the early eighties, as a committed believer called with a calling into uncharted waters, I was facing some unexpected challenges. I was grounded in God's Word, but operating beyond my natural abilities. My pastor imparted some advice that I didn't understand at the time, but that I heeded. His advice was to take three or four days alone with the Lord and do nothing but pray in the Spirit. I found that easier said than done, but I pressed through and emerged changed. That change might best be described as the gate to the bridge crossing the dividing asunder between soul and spirit. It provided and provides the release tied to the gifts Paul describes in Romans 12 that operationally were previously only trickles comparatively.

The gateway is that leap of faith we consciously take, after counting the costs, into what the scripture describes as walking in the spirit.

"If we live in the Spirit, let us also walk in the Spirit." Galatians 5:25

The Amplified version of Hebrews 4:12 reveals: *"Every word that God speaks is quick and powerful and sharper than any two-edged sword, piercing even to the division between soul and spirit."* The dividing asunder between soul and spirit is simultaneously the battleground and the bridge into the supernatural. It is the narrow path into the arena where the Kingdom of God reigns and brings the kingdom of darkness to its knees.

It's the path in which we lead by serving, we live by dying, we advance by yielding, we gain by giving. In God's kingdom, wisdom comes from simplicity, honor is a byproduct of humility, and order comes from change. It's in our weakness and humility that God's strength is manifested most fully.

It's the simple things that confound the wise. The narrow gate into God's Kingdom defines a pathway marked by the power of God. The power of God is predicated on hearing the voice of the Lord and obeying. It is the dividing asunder between what we can do for God and what we allow Him to do through us.

"Are you so foolish? After beginning with the Spirit, are you now trying to attain your goal by human effort? Have you suffered so much for nothing — if it really was for nothing? Does God give you his Spirit and work miracles among you because you observe the law, or because you believe what you heard?"
Galatians 3:3-5 NIV

CHAPTER 27

THE LEADERSHIP MEASURE

"For I say to you, that unless your righteousness exceeds the righteousness of the scribes and Pharisees, you will by no means enter the kingdom of heaven." Matthew 5:20

Jesus came not to dismantle the Law of Moses and the Prophets, but to fulfill them. Within that very context, He challenged the practices of the religious leaders.

"No one sews a piece of unshrunk cloth on an old garment; or else the new piece pulls away from the old, and the tear is made worse. And no one puts new wine into old wineskins; or else the new wine bursts the wineskins, the wine is spilled, and the wineskins are ruined. But new wine must be put into new wineskins." Mark 2:21-22

Jesus broke the mold. Despite going against the grain of the Pharisees' conventions, He was not suggesting anarchy. He was addressing something more.

Over the centuries the devil has been busy penetrating the ranks of spiritual leadership in his efforts to redefine the order established by the Law and the Prophets. Jesus came to destroy the works of the devil. His mission served to restore God's order.

The Point of Stumbling

At issue was and is the gauge of success and the measure of leadership that differentiates churchianity from revival-driven, societal transformation. The principal point of stumbling by the religious leaders perverted power and impeded the true leadership that marks the Kingdom. That point of stumbling was blind conformity.

"Take heed what you hear. For with the same measure you use, it will be measured to you; and to you who hear, more will be given. For whoever has, to him more will be given; but whoever does not have, even what he has will be taken away." Mark 4: 24-25

In the late fifties a book titled *"The Organization Man"* was the rage. Its message was that the pathway to success, corporately, was through corporate conformity. Today, in the political arenas, a similar overlay guiding the conformity of issues has emerged from "political correctness."

In the Church, the adherence to group-think has had its own variation of the "organization man." Perpetuated by the dichotomy between the sacred and secular, along with the separation of the priests and the laity, the mobilization intended by *"perfecting the saints for the work of the ministry"* is undermined.

The gap between the sacred and secular; and the priests and the laity strategically minimizes the impact of the believing community on the world around it. It was one of the central misguided myths that Jesus came to restore. The role of Kingdom leaders is to replicate themselves and mobilize the community rather than repel them.

"So Jesus said to them, surely tax collectors and harlots will enter the kingdom of God before you. Therefore, the kingdom of God will be taken from you and given to a people bearing the fruits of it." Matthew 21:31, 44

When Jesus said He was not replacing the Law and the Prophets, but fulfilling them, it bore on extending the mantle of leadership to those who would break the mold, take up the mantle of the Kingdom, wield change and go beyond the limited, myopic scope demonstrated by the Pharisees.

His reference was to a standard of leadership that incorporated both modeling and imparting the principles of God's truth.

*"Whoever therefore breaks one of the least of these commandments, and teaches men so, shall be called least in the kingdom of heaven; but **whoever does and teaches** them, he shall be called great in the kingdom of heaven."* Matthew 5:18-19

The Leadership Priority

The organization man in the Church is the product of replacing mentoring leaders with an organizational paradigm that distorts true Kingdom leadership. True leadership begins by example, but then extends to preparing others with the same mantle to lead. It is a process rather than a goal. It is the means by which the community of believers grows and extends the influence of change to those around it.

"This is the will of God, that by your good works you will put to silence the ignorance of foolish men." 1 Peter 2:15

Leadership is a function, long before it becomes a position. True leadership is based on influence. The counterfeit is power. True leadership may result in a position, but position is in reality secondary, and only then a means to an end. The early church was viewed as turning the world upside down. That was a function of influence, not position. Joseph's function as a slave was described with the words: *"everyone saw that the Lord was with Joseph and made all that he did to prosper."* Then while in prison, the jailer entrusted him with his authority because he saw God operating through Joseph.

"The LORD was with Joseph and showed him mercy, and gave him favor in the sight of the keeper of the prison, who committed to Joseph's hand all the prisoners in the prison. He did not look into anything that was under Joseph's authority, because the LORD was with him; and whatever he did, the LORD made it prosper." Genesis 39:21-23

Each believer has a sphere of influence. It stems from the authority of God operating within them. True leadership engenders trust and is the gateway for wielding the influence for God's authority.

The issue bears on what rules and governs the standards by which society lives. The Organization Man is driven by the "rule of profit." Political correctness creates a following governed by adherence to particular issues based on a particular "rule of power."

When the church defines its standards by the rule of profit, political correctness or any other standard other than the Word of God, it succumbs to the lesser order, which undermines the rule of the Kingdom.

*"Whoever therefore breaks one of the least of these commandments, and teaches men so, shall be called least in the kingdom of heaven; but **whoever does and teaches** them, he shall be called great in the kingdom of heaven."* Matthew 5:18-19

The Conformity Trap

Blind conformity emasculates leadership as God intended and perpetuates the status quo. It minimizes the potential for impact from the community of God's people. Jesus' reference to the religious leaders as whitewashed walls and hypocrites points to their role of leadership falling short; of there being something essential and key that they had missed altogether.

"Woe to you, scribes and Pharisees, hypocrites! For you shut up the kingdom of heaven against men; for you neither go in yourselves, nor do you allow those who are entering to go in." Matthew 23:13-14

In addressing blind conformity that keeps God's people bound and anemic, Jesus made it clear that there would be hurdles to challenging the status quo. It's why He described the Kingdom path as being narrow and difficult. The Kingdom pathway goes against the grain. Yet, this is the very path from which to release the captives, give sight to the blind and free the oppressed. It is the foundation for activating times of God's favor.

"The Spirit of the Lord is upon me to preach the good news to the poor, to proclaim release to the captives, give sight to the blind, free the oppressed and proclaim the favorable year of the Lord." Luke 4:18-19

God's favor, the release of His Spirit to the level of what we refer to as revival, comes when the mold is broken and God's people, each within their own spheres, begin finding the freedom that God has intended all along. Yet, the people are described as sheep without a shepherd and the leaders deemed as blind guides. So it is until the mold of conformity is replaced with a righteousness that exceeds the leadership of the scribes and Pharisees, we will not see the release of the Kingdom to manifest societal change.

The Righteousness That Exceeds

The "righteousness that exceeds" pivots on the tz'dakah. Tz'dakah, as righteous charity, builds the community. It underlies the premise of servant leadership outlined by Jesus. In short, it is the community dynamic that takes care of its own.

Isaiah describes this tz'dakah-righteousness. He says that the fruit of righteousness (tz'dakah) will be peace and effect of righteousness will be quietness and confidence forever. Certainly, the limited interpretation of righteousness by the church as a higher ethical standard has yet to bring this level of result.

When Jesus said *"whoever does and teaches [these principles] shall be called great in the Kingdom of heaven,"* he was giving reference to the influence to be wielded by each within their own sphere. It was the premise by which the book of Moses said that the community of God's people would be *"the head and not the tail; to bring increase and not decrease."* (Deuteronomy 28:13)

The Measure of Increase

One of the chief deceptions and challenges, as leaders, is applying the right measures.

Kingdom leadership pivots on influence. Whereas it begins with priorities, those priorities first require embracing the right model. With the right model will come the right influence; the influence with the "Kingdom measure." That measure is increase. Yet, it is not the standard of increase according to the world's measure, although it may incorporate it. But it also may not.

God's Word incorporates the model. Abraham ran a God-centered, entrepreneurial community. Deuteronomy outlines the principles of how God's people should govern and bring increase and blessing to the world they live in. The impact of the influence from this model wielded by the Jewish people has shaped the development of Western society.

Yet, from a human perspective, relegating God to a benign position in the course of politically-correct world-events has perverted the model and the pathway it is designed to uncover. God's truth will always exceed the wisdom of this world. However, without His Spirit at the operational center, His truth will digress into the confines of intellectual debate, which was the very trap that had ensnared the Pharisees.

There is a keen difference between the "rule of profit" and God's increase; as well as the "rule of power" and God's measure of leadership.

The measure of God's leadership brings increase and life to those around them. It is being blessed to be a blessing, like Joseph, so that all-the-world recognizes that God is with us. Increase is at the heart of the very strategy of leadership that Moses outlined in Deuteronomy to guide the community of God's people into becoming the head and not the tail.

"When you harvest your field and overlook a sheaf, do not go back to get it. Leave it for the foreigner, the fatherless and the widow, so that the Lord may bless you in all the work of your hands. When you beat the olives from your trees or harvest the grapes in your vineyards, do not go over the branches a second time." Deut 24: 18-21

Jesus both modeled and taught this strategy of increase with His approach to mentoring His disciples. It is the measure for leadership conforming to the community standard for stewardship that He summed up in His command to train the nations in Matthew 28; or to use the common translation of *"make disciples of the nations."* It evolves from the Ephesians 4 mobilization of perfecting the saints for the ministry that brings increase.

"The things which you have heard from me in the presence of many witnesses, entrust these to faithful men, who will be able to teach others also." 2 Timothy 2:2

This measure of increase in operation by Jesus' followers, aptly illustrating the parable of the talents, was described by a non-believer in Acts 17 as *"turning the world upside down."* God's very DNA is to create, to innovate, to build and to multiply; to bring increase. It's the priority that actuates the model for influence. It is the leadership measure by which the Kingdom is advanced and revival released.

In short, the simplicity of a mature, mobilized Body, growing as they mentor others, will release Kingdom authority for transformation. Its result will bring increase in the magnitude of the exponential. It is the catalyst for the release of the unharnessed fire of God. It is a byproduct of the balanced stewardship we have as God's people in ruling over the work of His hands. It marks the narrow path and foundation for influence and change by which we will release the captives, turn the world upside down and actuate the time of God's favor.

"Do not think that I came to destroy the Law or the Prophets. I did not come to destroy but to fulfill. For assuredly, I say to you, till heaven and earth pass away, one jot or one tittle will by no means pass from the law till all is fulfilled." Matthew 5:17

CHAPTER 28

THE HEART OF A KING

"When the first came, they supposed that they would receive more. When they had received the same, they complained saying, 'These last men have worked only one hour, and we have borne the burden and the heat of the day.' But he answered, 'friend, did you not agree on this amount? Take what is yours and go your way. I wish to give this last man the same as you. Is it not lawful for me to do what I wish with what I own? Or is your eye evil because I am good?' So the last will be first, and the first last. For many are called, but few chosen." Matthew 20: 10-16

This parable is part of a sequence of teachings on the Kingdom of God. It follows the story of passing through the eye of the needle as an illustration of the difficulty for a rich man entering the Kingdom. It includes Jesus' admonition to the young ruler to sell all that he had to reorient his priorities as a prelude to becoming Jesus' follower. It precedes His teaching on serving being the foundation to true greatness.

What follows then is the parable of the two sons working in their father's vineyard; then the very strong statement Jesus made to the scribes and Pharisee about having the Kingdom taken from them and given to a people bearing the fruits of it.

The theme of entering the Kingdom and bearing fruit differentiates believers from followers. It explains the difference between the called and the chosen in the opening parable, as well as the hurdles for the rich man in Matthew 19. The issue bears not on our salvation, but to the Kingdom role that we as individuals, as well as a Body are to play out on the earth. It is the basis for what the Apostle Paul described in Ephesians 4 of not being tossed to and fro like children.

It is at the heart of the parable of the sheep and the goats.

"Then the King will say to those on His right hand, 'Come, you blessed of My Father, inherit the kingdom prepared for you from the foundation of the world: for I was hungry and you gave Me food; I was thirsty and you gave Me drink; I was a stranger and you took Me in; I was naked and you clothed Me; I was sick and you visited Me; I was in prison and you came to Me.' Then the righteous will answer Him, saying, 'Lord, when did we feed You, take You in, or clothe You? He will answer them, 'In as much as you did it to one of the least of these My brethren, you did it to Me.'" Matthew 25: 37-46

Beyond the dichotomy between the social gospel and the gospel of salvation is the issue in Matthew 20:16 bearing on, not our salvation, but the calling we have as His followers in serving in His vineyard: in the Kingdom.

So the last will be first, and the first last. For many are called, but few chosen."

The Focus

The Kingdom message for most in the church has come to be reduced to the hereafter and what will unfold in the millennium, while we acquiesce to living within the parameters being outlined by the world.

Jesus came to restore the foundations. He came to seek and save that which was lost at Adam's "fall." Introducing His earthly ministry with the words: *"The Kingdom of God is at hand,"* His core message unveiled the principles needed to operate in the Kingdom.

Functionally, Jesus laid an axe to the root of the subtle alliance between the religious elite and the rulers of the worldly realm. Simultaneously, He closed the gap between God and every-day people. The result was the restoration of the role of God's people being a light to the world with the biblical spiritual, economic and community dynamic. He repeatedly demonstrated Kingdom authority and modeled the heart needed to bring reality to the calling. Then He passed the mantle to His followers.

The principles Jesus imparted reestablished the foundations for true leadership. They mark the pathway whereby the authority of God brings the change to become the government of God. It is the gateway into the supernatural that brings societal transformation. It is what Jesus described as the narrow path because it didn't follow the enticement to "be like everyone else." Jesus recalibrated the equation that restored God's intention for His people to be blessed to be a blessing. From this function comes the seedbed from which His Kingdom grows.

Jesus not only prepared His followers with the principles to establish His Kingdom, but He mapped out the dynamics of the pathway for those embracing the destiny of the chosen.

In Matthew 28 Jesus said: *"Go and make disciples of all nations, teaching them to observe all I have commanded you."* This mandate was entrusted to a small contingent of some of the most unlikely followers. It embraced the mandate God had given to man at creation: dominion.

The Original Mandate

God created man to exercise dominion over all the earth.

The fall of man would impact the way dominion would be implemented. Despite wide swings in the use and misuse of power, God's original intention has been punctuated by key individuals who have ushered in societal transformation marked by God at the center.

The Apostle Paul captured the dynamic in his letter to the Romans: *"creation itself longs for the revealing of the sons of God that it might be delivered from the bondage of corruption as it gains entrance into this glorious freedom."*

The God-Centered Culture

The original mandate and Jesus' Matthew 28 mandate point to something more than our Western focus of the gospel. It's where the gospel of salvation and the social gospel collide: with the gospel of the Kingdom. It is the gospel that people run to because they see the reality and demonstration of God operating in their midst. It is the gospel where God is at the center of everyday life.

The Church that started out as being described as *"turning the world upside down,"* waned in the original mandate for God's people exercising dominion over the work of His hands. Still, the Church has spread the spiritual precepts of the faith to the ends of the earth.

On the other hand, over the centuries of the Diaspora, the Jewish people have contributed to and exercised the influence to society around them that has shaped the governmental, economic, justice and the moral standards of Western society. Yet, despite the temptation for many to "be like everyone else," as a people they have maintained their unique identity.

At the heart of the remarkable impact the Jewish people have made on Western civilization has been the principles contained in the Five Books of Moses. These are the principles governing the economic community model operated by Abraham. Jesus elaborated on these truths, demonstrating and imparting through them, the keys to how the Kingdom of God operates. His purpose was to restore the intent God had at the beginning: for his people to rule over the work of His hands.

Bearing the Fruits

Moses' father-in-law Jethro unveiled the distinction between the principles, the pathway and the work tied to our callings, as being foundational to leadership.

"Teach them the principles and precepts; then show them the pathway in which they must walk for the work that they must do." Exodus 18:20

Central to what Jesus imparted to His followers on the Kingdom was the connection between stewardship and righteousness; and between leadership and service. The parable of the man with two sons is an indictment against those designated as heirs, who pass through the gates, but who don't have a grasp of the pathway or priorities to their true calling. They confuse building their own empire at the gates with bearing fruit for the Kingdom.

"A man had two sons, and he came to the first and said, 'Son, go, work today in my vineyard.' He answered and said, 'I will not,' but afterward he regretted it and went. He went to the second son and said likewise. He answered him, 'I go, sir,' but he did not go. Which of the two did the will of his father? They said to Him, 'The first.' So, Jesus said to them: surely, tax collectors and harlots will enter the kingdom of God before you." Matthew 21: 28-31

The parable of the talents demonstrates the pivotal emphasis to be given to stewardship, to bringing increase, within the framework of *"each according to his own ability."* The separation of the sheep and goats bears on Jesus' word to the religious hypocrites that *the Kingdom of God would be taken from them and given to a people bearing the fruits of the Kingdom.* (Matthew 21: 43)

Something More

As God's people, we have had the Truth. However, apart from those we refer to as the heroes of faith, the application of the Truth has fallen short of what *"creation itself has longed for."* In the course of our everyday lives, dominion seems to either elude us or to take a back seat to the straining of gnats as the over-spiritualizing Pharisees did.

"So the last will be first, and the first last. For many are called, but few chosen." Matthew 20:16

In our zeal we cry out for that "something more." There indeed is a deep longing to see the Truth we wield consistently converging with the dynamic that enabled the models of faith from times past. Joseph the Patriarch demonstrated it under the most adverse of circumstances. Daniel exercised it when immersed in a culture of sorcery. David, as a most unlikely candidate, prevailed with it and ushered His people into a time of great unity and peace. Jesus made it the central message of His earthly ministry.

So, what is the catalyst? What distinguishes His followers from being in the world, but not of the world? What is it that ignites the flame that consistently bears fruit worthy of repentance; that results in those known by His Name being considered the "righteous," who bring the type of change that marks the difference between the called and chosen?

The Catalyst

In short, Jesus prepared and released His followers to operate with the heart of a king.

A recent movie, "The Gladiator," illustrates the significance tied to a kingly heart. The hero of the story is a famous Roman General, who became a slave and a gladiator. His kingly character was always recognized regardless of his rank or position. In the end, he did more for the Rome he loved as a slave/gladiator than he had ever done as a conquering General.

Those anointed to lead among God's people are those who employ a genuine kingly heart for the community they lead. Jesus' followers are those tasked with picking up His mantle to bring dominion and establish God's Kingdom rule. They do so within the economic community dimensions of where people live their lives.

"Jesus said to them, peace to you! As the Father has sent Me, so I also send you." John 20:21

Embracing the kingly heart that brings dominion must first ensure it avoids the type of heart that perverts its authority. Proverbs 30 provides keen insight into the positional deceptions to the kingly heart. It says: *"Under three things the earth trembles, under four it cannot bear up: a slave when he becomes king, and a fool when glutted with food; an unloved woman when she gets a husband and a maid when she succeeds her mistress."*

The king who has the heart of a slave is one who misuses authority. The leader who has a heart of a fool is ruled by desires. The one in charge without love will never trust and the ruler with an oppressed heart will pervert authority. These elements congeal into what scripture refers to as *"the bondage of corruption"* or what we commonly refer to as the abuse of power.

The Kingly Mantle

The mark of true leadership is not position, but influence. Despite Joseph and Daniel being slaves, they never succumbed to a slave's heart. They operated with the heart of a king. They demonstrated the reality of God in a way that all those around them recognized the blessings that flowed through them as coming from God.

A true king is not determined by position or wealth, but by his heart. A king is one who not only brings influence, but serves as a catalyst for opportunity that brings blessing to those in his realm. A true king builds and replicates. A true king mobilizes others to enable opportunity that breathes life into not only individuals, but the impact made on the community.

The heart of a king in God's Kingdom is significantly different from that of the world. That's what Jesus drilled into His followers. Their kingly roles began with their identity in God and manifested through the unique expressions of the gifts of the Spirit, each of which have their basis in serving.

The lynchpin of a king's heart is honor. A king's heart reflects a character of honor. Without honor, the one in the role of king is only serving a position. It is the quest Jesus addressed with Martha, who being distracted with all her activities, was admonished to getting her priorities right (Luke 10:38).

The one called to operate with the heart of the King cannot be like everyone else. Worldly rulers are driven by ego, passions, power, their lusts and ambition. The Kingdom operates on a completely different premise. On the surface these dynamics seem contradictory to their intent, but in reality they are the keys to the Kingdom. *We lead by serving. We advance by yielding. Honor comes through humility. Wisdom is found in simplicity. Making your assets multiply will bring promotion. Growth comes by giving to others. We extend love to our enemies. Our purpose in life comes through giving it up. We receive when giving. Perfect love eliminates fear. In our weakness we are made strong. Ownership increases by sharing. We bless those who curse us.*

Kingdom leadership wields power in a manner unlike the world. Its impact is derived from far more than natural ability, with its authority recognized as coming from God.

Alignment with God's Heart

Many are called, but few will be chosen. It involves an alignment with God reflecting not one vestige of variation between His will and our will. Jesus said, *"I and my Father are one."* The cost pivots on truly knowing God's heart and entering that place where it is not what we do for God, but rather what we allow God to do through us.

"It is no longer I who lives, but Christ who lives in me." Gal 2:20.

Those with this calling will mobilize the community into oneness with God's heart. This mobilization will be more than revival. It will result in God being released through the community of believers who bear His heart. While revival is marked by men's hearts drawn to God, a move of God extends beyond, to the level that impacts and brings change to society. Revival is the spark, while a movement is the fire of God.

Many are called, but few are chosen. David was described as a man after God's own heart. He was able to bring God's people together in unity because he sought God's heart and yielded himself to it. It is why, when Jesus returns, He will sit on the throne of David to rule over His Kingdom. It is because David employed his kingly mantle to bring the community of God's people together into harmony with God's heart.

Joseph bore the cost to take on God's heart and the heart of a king. That mantle of kingly leadership was acknowledged and connected to God while He was yet a slave and despite him being in prison. His kingly heart impacted everyone around him. When his interview came with Pharaoh, Pharaoh recognized Joseph's mantle and a heart undeniably tied to God.

Joseph, Moses, David and Daniel modeled the kingly heart. They each changed the course of nations. They each broke the mold and in the face of adversity, gave birth to opportunity. Jesus, confronting the alliance of death between the politically correct religious elite and the worldly power brokers, released a trans-generational movement that has been transforming the course of nations.

Before us is a time when the gap is being closed between the purposes of God and the power structures of this world. From today's emerging generation of believers will come leaders willing to pay the cost. These are ones whose success will be derived from far more than ability, whose charisma extends beyond performance. They will be ones bearing the heart of a king and the anointing of the King. They are the ones who will impart God's heart to the community of His people and usher in the move of God that will bring back the King of kings. As the community of God's people embrace His heart in unity, the shift of all ages will move into place.

"Then the kingdoms of this world will become the kingdoms of our Lord and he shall reign for ever." Rev.21: 10

The Kingdom of God is at hand. The longing of all creation will yield its fruit as the sons of God assume their kingly hearts; pick up their mantles and the Kingdom manifests.

"What is man that You take thought of him, and the son of man that You care for him? Yet You have made him a little lower than God, and You crown him with glory and majesty! You make him to rule over the works of Your hands; You have put all things under his feet..." Psalm 8:4-6 NASU

AUTHOR
Morris E. Ruddick

Entrepreneur, consultant, minister and business owner, Morris Ruddick has led development of entrepreneurial activities in critical needy areas and brought together combined business-ministry initiatives in several nations, with a focus on assisting believers in lands of persecution and distress. Mr. Ruddick's Kingdom agendas reflect a unique merging of the secular and the spiritual with initiatives based on biblical principles of business. Since 1995, he has been at the forefront of encouraging and mobilizing spiritually-minded business leaders to step out in faith by combining their entrepreneurial and spiritual gifts to build communities and impact their nations.

In the last few years Mr. Ruddick's Kingdom agendas have spanned five continents with hands-on activities in Russia, Belarus, Nigeria, Ethiopia, Botswana, Afghanistan, China, Vietnam and Israel. His Kingdom business initiatives have included entrepreneurial startup programs, training for spiritual business leaders and community building strategies for lands of persecution and oppression. His programs are based on the biblical model of sowing and reaping in famine. He helped organize and launch, and continues serving as board member for the Joseph Project, an Israeli-based international consortium of humanitarian aid that assists Israeli immigrants and citizens.

Israel's Technology Incubator Program is listed among the clients he has served. He is a former board member of the Nehemiah Fund, an Israeli non-profit (amuta) that has provided grants to members of Israel's believing community facing economic distress.

Mr. Ruddick served 19 years on the board of Marilyn Hickey Ministries and Orchard Road Christian Center where he was Chairman of both the Compensation and Audit Committees. He is a member of the Messianic Jewish Alliance. He served as Corporate Secretary of the International Christian Chamber of Commerce-USA and is a board member of Love Botswana Outreach. He has been a national speaker and workshop leader for the National Religious Broadcasters, Mike and Cindy Jacob's Out of the Box Marketplace Conferences, the GCOWE Missions Conference, Os Hillman's Marketplace Ministry Leader's Summit, Peter Wagner's Roundtable on Kingdom Wealth, the Kingdom Economic Yearly Summit (KEYS); and as a part of the editorial advisory board of the *Journal of Ministry Marketing and Management*.

Over the years, he has served executive suite management with his planning and strategy development talents in a diversity of progressive mid-sized operations, ministry groups, and Fortune 500 companies. He has been at the helm of designing and implementing two successful corporate turnarounds, one being for a $1.4 billion firm. He holds ordination papers from the United Christian Ministerial Association, a BS from Northwestern University; and an MS in communications and doctoral work in statistics; as well as a year of biblical studies at Oral Roberts University.

CONTACT INFORMATION

To contact the author
to speak at your conference or gathering of marketplace leaders,
please write

Morris Ruddick
Global Initiatives Foundation
P.O. Box 370291
Denver, CO 80237 USA

or email:

info@strategic-initiatives.org

or call 303.741-9000 and leave a message

You may wish to visit the Global Initiatives Foundation website. It contains additional articles and information. The website address is:

http://www.strategic-initiatives.org

Breinigsville, PA USA
16 February 2010
232614BV00002B/2/P